Scientific Writing for Psychology

Second Edition

Sara Miller McCune founded SAGE Publishing in 1965 to support the dissemination of usable knowledge and educate a global community. SAGE publishes more than 1000 journals and over 800 new books each year, spanning a wide range of subject areas. Our growing selection of library products includes archives, data, case studies and video. SAGE remains majority owned by our founder and after her lifetime will become owned by a charitable trust that secures the company's continued independence.

Los Angeles | London | New Delhi | Singapore | Washington DC | Melbourne

Scientific Writing for Psychology

Lessons in Clarity and Style

Second Edition

Robert V. Kail

Purdue University

Los Angeles | London | New Delhi
Singapore | Washington DC | Melbourne

FOR INFORMATION:

SAGE Publications, Inc.
2455 Teller Road
Thousand Oaks, California 91320
E-mail: order@sagepub.com

SAGE Publications Ltd.
1 Oliver's Yard
55 City Road
London EC1Y 1SP
United Kingdom

SAGE Publications India Pvt. Ltd.
B 1/I 1 Mohan Cooperative Industrial Area
Mathura Road, New Delhi 110 044
India

SAGE Publications Asia-Pacific Pte Ltd
18 Cross Street #10-10/11/12
China Square Central
Singapore 048423

Printed in the United States of America

Library of Congress Cataloging-in-Publication Data

Names: Kail, Robert V., author.

Title: Scientific writing for psychology : lessons in clarity and style / Robert V. Kail, Purdue University.

Description: Second edition. | Los Angeles : SAGE, [2019] | Includes bibliographical references and index.

Identifiers: LCCN 2018040488 | ISBN 9781544309620 (pbk. : alk. paper)

Subjects: LCSH: Psychology—Authorship. | Technical writing—Vocational guidance.

Classification: LCC BF76 .K35 2019 | DDC 808.06/615—dc23 LC record available at https://lccn.loc.gov/2018040488

This book is printed on acid-free paper.

Acquisitions Editor: Lara Parra
Editorial Assistant: Drew Fabricius
Production Editor: Astha Jaiswal
Copy Editor: Mark Bast
Typesetter: Hurix Digital
Proofreader: Ellen Howard
Indexer: Diggs Publishing Services
Cover Designer: Ginkhan Siam
Marketing Manager: Katherine Hepburn

18 19 20 21 22 10 9 8 7 6 5 4 3 2 1

Brief Contents

Detailed Contents

4 | The Art of Fine Paragraphs   49

5 | Framing an Introduction   69

6 | Reporting Results

7 | Discussing Your Findings

Acknowledgments

I became interested in scientific writing during my first course in experimental psychology (more than 40 years ago!) at Ohio Wesleyan University. Students were required to prepare several reports of research we had conducted. I remember thinking that my first report was "pretty good" and being crestfallen when it came back covered with red ink marking spots that were wordy, vague, or just plain wrong. My teachers in that experimental course—Harry Bahrick, Harvey Freeman, and Roy Wittlinger—provided the first lessons in a lifelong education in the ways of writing clearly and persuasively. Those lessons were followed by more advanced instruction and more red ink from my graduate advisors at the University of Michigan, John Hagen and Harold Stevenson. Thanks to all these people for their tutelage and for encouraging me to pursue psychology as a career.

Many years later I began writing a textbook in child psychology and had the opportunity to work with two outstanding manuscript editors, Harriett Prentiss and Susan Moss. They showed me many tips for making my writing engaging and inviting, tips that appear in this book. I'll always be grateful for their insights. And a special thanks to Harriett for introducing me to *Style* by Joseph M. Williams (2000); his insights on writing are inspirational and drive many of my recommendations for effective writing.

More recently, I was fortunate to serve as editor of *Psychological Science*, the flagship journal of the Association for Psychological Science. During my 5-year term, I read about 10,000 manuscripts. Many were models of straightforward scientific writing—clear and concise with an important take-home message. I'm grateful to these authors for helping me to recognize the essential elements of a well-crafted scientific report and for motivating many of the examples that appear throughout this book.

Unfortunately, I also read several papers that fell short of this mark: They were wordy not concise, confusing not clear, and obscure not direct. These manuscripts led me to create a short course on scientific writing for graduate students in psychology. Teaching the course helped me identify fundamental lessons for novice scientific writers and convinced me that a book based on these lessons would be valuable.

I'm grateful to Reid Hester and Lara Parra for their support of this book, to Mark Bast for cleaning the prose, to Anne Bridgman for her feedback on the illustrative manuscript that appears in the Epilogue, and to Astha Jaiswal for shepherding the project through production.

Finally, I thank my wife, Dea, for sharing my enthusiasm when my writing was going well and for tolerating my pessimism when it wasn't.

Robert V. Kail

About the Author

Robert V. Kail is Distinguished Professor of Psychological Sciences at Purdue University. His undergraduate degree is from Ohio Wesleyan University, and his PhD is from the University of Michigan. He received the McCandless Young Scientist Award from the American Psychological Association, was named the Distinguished Sesquicentennial Alumnus in Psychology by Ohio Wesleyan University, is a fellow of the Association for Psychological Science, and is an honorary professor at the University of Heidelberg, Germany.

Prologue

Scientific psychologists need to write well to communicate their findings with others, but their training typically includes few opportunities to master this skill. Undergraduate psychology majors are first exposed to scientific writing in a research methods course, where they write reports of research conducted in class. Some undergraduates later write a senior thesis, and as graduate students they write a master's thesis or a doctoral dissertation. These are all valuable experiences, but they are insufficient to allow students to become masters. After all, athletes or musicians who have a similar level of experience are considered novices; they've just started the long trip to mastery.

My goal in this book is to help you improve your scientific writing. I view scientific writing as a skill, a view that has two implications for the book. First, in most skills, experts often know "tools of the trade"—strategies, tips, heuristics—that work. This book is designed to teach you some of the tools that expert authors use to make their writing seem clear, concise, cohesive, and compelling. Second, like most skills, learning to write well requires massive amounts of practice—10,000 hours is commonly cited as the amount of practice needed to become an expert in many domains. This book includes exercises that will allow you to practice your craft without having to wait until your next opportunity to prepare a full-fledged research report.

The book is organized around seven lessons: three devoted to sentences, one to paragraphs, and three to writing research reports. In each lesson, I describe tools that experts use to write effective sentences, paragraphs, and reports. In addition, each lesson includes exercises that allow you to try out the tools and ends with "For Practice," which suggests ways to improve your writing by looking at strengths and weaknesses of published articles.

This is not a book to be read in one setting; the book's real value for you is in doing the exercises. Just as athletes master skills by practicing them (not by reading about them), you need to do the exercises to improve your writing. With that said, let's begin.[1]

---

[1] Throughout the book I use contractions because I want you to feel as if we're talking casually about writing. But don't use contractions in your scientific writing because most editors consider them too informal.

1

Writing Clearly

Researchers typically communicate their findings to the scientific community with written reports. Such reports are most valuable when readers can easily understand what the researchers discovered. Unfortunately, many reports published in scientific journals are not written clearly, making it difficult for other scientists to understand the contribution of the research that's being described. In this lesson, we'll see some of the typical obstacles to clear writing and learn how to avoid them.

To begin, suppose you had asked me to describe what I did for lunch today. I might write the following:

(1a) After returning from the gym, I had my usual lunch: a sandwich, an apple, and a Diet Coke.

Alternatively, I might describe lunch like this:

(1b) After a return from the site of physical activity, consumption of a sandwich, an apple, and a Diet Coke was accomplished by me.

Had I written sentence 1b you probably would have thought me pompous, pretentious, or just plain strange. Yet when writers move from writing about lunch to writing about research, too often they abandon the straightforward style of sentence 1a in favor of the stilted text of sentence 1b.

Consider this pair of sentences:

(2a) The demonstration of contextual influence on visual perception is the primary contribution of this report.

(2b) Our primary finding is that context influences how people perceive visual stimuli.

Sentence 2a is the sort of sentence that's common in reports published in psychological journals, but sentence 2b expresses the same idea in language that's more direct and easier to understand.

Similarly, compare sentences 3a and 3b.

(3a) Overestimation of negative reactions to unpleasant outcomes is common because of underestimation of adjustment to those outcomes.

(3b) People often overestimate how negatively they will respond to unpleasant outcomes because they underestimate their ability to adjust to those outcomes.

The idea that's obscure in sentence 3a is crystal clear in sentence 3b.

In this lesson we'll see how to write sentences like 1a, 2b, and 3b, which are clear, concrete, and direct; and how to avoid sentences like 1b, 2a, and 3a, which are vague, abstract, and obscure. We'll start by looking at a primary symptom of obscure writing and then consider strategies for writing clearly.

WHAT MAKES SOME WRITING HARD TO READ?

Sentences 1b, 2a, and 3a represent a kind of writing that's often known as *bureaucratese* or *academese*, depending on the author's profession. The hallmark of such writing is the frequent presence of **nominalizations**[1], nouns derived from verbs or adjectives. For example, *organization, recruitment, prominence,* and *brightness* are nominalizations derived from verbs (*organize, recruit*) and adjectives (*prominent, bright*). Other nominalizations found frequently in psychological writing are shown in Table 1.

Nominalizations make writing seem obscure because they take the concrete action of a verb or the descriptive power of an adjective and bury it in a noun. Nominalizations are particularly harmful when they appear as the subject of a sentence, coupled with a weak verb, such as *is, are, seems,* or *has.* Sentence 3a illustrates this pattern: "Overestimation . . . is . . ."

---

[1] Technical terms appear in **bold face** and are defined in the Glossary.

TABLE 1　**Common Nominalizations**

Verb	Nominalization	Adjective	Nominalization
expect	expectation	precise	precision
perform	performance	clear	clarity
evaluate	evaluation	significant	significance
integrate	integration	different	difference

EXERCISE 1.1

Identify the nominalizations in sentences 1b, 2a, and 3a.

A key to clear writing is <u>recognizing nominalizations</u> and, when possible, returning them to their original state as a verb or adjective. In fact, eliminating unnecessary nominalizations may be the single most important step in making your writing more direct and clear.

STRATEGIES FOR WRITING CLEAR, DIRECT SENTENCES

Avoiding nominalizations is good advice but not particularly satisfying because it says "what not to do" instead of "what to do." Let's return to sentences 1a and 1b (page 1). Sentence 1b is difficult because of the nominalizations, but it's not the mere absence of nominalizations that makes sentence 1a so easy to understand. Instead, sentence 1a is clear because it's a one-sentence story about a person (me) and his actions (eating lunch). As stories go, it's not much; Steven Spielberg isn't about to call for the movie rights. But it's a story nonetheless; and like much better stories by J. K. Rowling, John Grisham, and Nicholas Sparks, it's readable because it focuses on a person acting.

Storytelling may seem far removed from scientific writing, but scientific writing typically has a tale to tell. Sentence 4a is written in academese:

(4a)　The belief of in-groups is that out-group members are less intelligent and less attractive.

It has a nominalization in its subject (*belief*) that's linked to a weak verb (*is*). But there's a story lurking underneath, one about in-groups and what they believe.

Consequently, we get something that's much clearer if we revise the sentence by placing actors in the grammatical subject and their actions in the verb:

(4b)   In-groups believe that out-group members are less intelligent and less attractive.

Sentences 5a and 5b show the same pattern:

(5a)   Susceptibility to the vanishing-ball illusion seems greater in individuals with ASD.

(5b)   Individuals with ASD are more susceptible to the vanishing-ball illusion.

Sentence 5b is easier to read because it puts actors in the subject and changes the nominalization to an adjective (*susceptibility* → *susceptible*).

The examples we've seen so far involve simple sentences that include little more than a subject, verb, and object. But the same principles follow when we move to more complex sentences that include, for example, dependent clauses like the one in sentence 6a:

(6a)   Although skepticism of people who have been misleading previously is common in older children, trust in others is more frequent in preschool children.

Sentence 6a begins with a long **dependent clause** about older children and then moves to the **independent clause** about preschool children. The clauses have the same structure: a **noun phrase** built around a nominalization

EXERCISE 1.2

In each sentence, first identify the nominalization, then revise with actions as verbs and actors as subjects.

1. Extraction of the gist of a scene is accomplished in a fraction of a second.
2. Counterfactual reasoning was the focus of our research.
3. Disclosure of personal information to friends is less common among East Asians than among Westerners.
4. ²Job performance is greater when workers build coalitions with coworkers.

---

² Items marked with an asterisk (*) do not have answers listed at the end of the chapter; this is so instructors may assign them.

that's linked to a weak verb: *skepticism of people . . . is* and *trust in others is.* We can make the sentence more active (and clearer) by revising to eliminate the nominalizations, replacing *skepticism* with *skeptical* and *trust* (as a noun) with *trust* (as a verb):

(6b)   Although older children are skeptical of people who have misled them previously, preschool children generally trust others.

Sentence 7a is even more complex:

(7a)   Given this inability to identify the long-term benefits of a positive family life, the present longitudinal investigation was conducted.

In this case, the introductory dependent clause has two nominalizations (*inability, benefits*), and the independent clause has one (*investigation*). By replacing them with verbs and adjectives, and adding actors for the verbs, the sentence becomes clearer.

(7b)   Because past research has been unable to determine whether a positive family life is beneficial in the long term, we investigated this issue longitudinally.

When you run into sentences that are even longer and more complex grammatically, the same approach works: find nominalizations, replace them with verbs or adjectives, and add actors to the verbs. That said, although sentences 6b and 7b may be improved over sentences 6a and 7a, they're far from being straightforward. In the next section we'll look at strategies for writing long sentences clearly.

WRITING LONG SENTENCES CLEARLY

Good storytelling focuses on actors and their actions: Good sentences get to actors quickly and link those actors strongly with their actions. To translate this principle into a tool for revising, remember that actors are typically introduced in the subject of a sentence; their actions are captured in the verb (and the objects of that verb). This leads directly to one rule of thumb: Effective sentences get to the subject quickly; they do not begin with long introductory clauses that force the reader to wonder what a sentence is about. Such clauses make sentences 6b and 7b hard to understand. For example, in 6b, the story is about preschool children's beliefs, yet the reader must plow through a long clause about older children's beliefs. Similarly, in sentence 7b the story is about the author's longitudinal study, but this surfaces only after a lengthy critique of the state of the literature.

If an introductory clause has more than five or six words, shorten it so that the reader gets to the actors sooner. For example, the introductory clause in 6c has only three words, down from 12 in 6b.

(6c)   Unlike older children, preschool children generally trust people who have misled them previously.

Another strategy is to eliminate the introductory clause completely, by moving it to the end of the sentence:

(7c)   We investigated this issue longitudinally because past research has been unable to determine whether a positive family life is beneficial in the long term.

A second rule of thumb is to move directly from subject to verb to object; unnecessary words inserted between the subject and verb or between verb and object weaken the links between the key elements in the story line. Sentence 8a demonstrates this problem:

(8a)   Some adults, due to attachment anxiety, are skeptical that spouses will support them in times of need.

EXERCISE 1.3

Revise these sentences to eliminate the long introductory clause.

* 1.   Because bilingual children have extensive experience selecting one language for production and inhibiting another, their cognitive control surpasses that of monolingual children.
2.   Although both white and black individuals experience anxiety during interracial interactions, people can detect such anxiety only in members of their own race.
3.   Given that studies have relied on different measures of narcissism and that samples have varied in the percentage of females who were included, we cannot determine whether today's college students are more narcissistic than prior students.
4.   *When couples reveal their feelings, address threats to their relationship, and rejoice in each other's accomplishments, their relationship grows stronger.

The story is about adults who doubt that spouses will support them. The actor, _adults, is the subject of the sentence_, and the action, _are skeptical_, is the **verb phrase**. But inserting _due to attachment anxiety_ between subject and verb separates the actor from the actions. Fixing this one is easy:

> (8b) Due to attachment anxiety, some adults are skeptical that
> spouses will support them in times of need.

Due to attachment anxiety works fine as an introductory clause because it's only four words long. And removing it from the independent clause strengthens the link between the subject and verb.

Phrases inserted between verbs and objects are just as disruptive:

> (9a) Experiencing power enhances, across diverse cultures, people's
> satisfaction with their friendships, romantic relationships,
> and jobs.

The story line about the impact of power on life satisfaction is interrupted by a phrase, _across diverse cultures_, that deals with generality of the phenomenon. Here, too, moving the phrase to the beginning of the sentence solves the problem:

> (9b) Across diverse cultures, experiencing power enhances people's
> satisfaction with their friendships, romantic relationships,
> and jobs.

Sometimes long sentences aren't clear because they sprawl. Despite a solid core in which subject, verb, and object are linked well, the sentence goes on

EXERCISE 1.4

Identify and relocate the disruptive text.

1. The size and orientation of an object affect, via pathways in visual and motor cortex, how people grasp it.
2. Unconscious thinking, for a range of problems, leads to better solutions.
3. People are quite skilled, despite remembering exact pitch inaccurately, at remembering patterns of changes in pitches.
4. *Competition between groups, according to this theory, leads individuals to acquire their group's norms.

and on. One clause is piled on top of another, almost as if the author kept adding new thoughts while writing. Sentence 10a illustrates sprawl:

(10a)   Most studies of age-related differences in processing speed have relied on samples of children living in developed nations, which may bias conclusions about the size of age-related differences, although research on other topics conducted with samples from developed nations has sometimes led to findings that generalize to developing nations.

The sentence starts fine, with a story about age differences in processing speed. It sprawls as it mentions a potential problem in this research but then suggests that the problem may not be worrisome after all.[3]

The first step in eliminating sentence sprawl is to remember the story line and drop text that doesn't contribute. In sentence 10a, the remark about other research on the topic seems unrelated and could be deleted:

(10b)   Most studies of age-related differences in processing speed have relied on samples of children living in developed nations, which may bias conclusions about the size of age-related differences.

Sentence 10b is better but can be improved further. To see how, we need to focus on *which*, a **relative pronoun** that, like any pronoun, needs an antecedent. In sentences such as 10b, the antecedent of *which* is sometimes not obvious and readers must search for it, a process that delays their comprehension momentarily. A trick for handling such sentences is to replace *which* with its antecedent and the word *that*. For example, sentence 11a includes a dependent clause that begins with *which*:

(11a)   Some hints about the impact of emotion on perception come from research on the attentional-blink paradigm, which shows that people identify emotionally significant words faster than neutral words.

We can replace *which* with its antecedent—*research*—and *that*:

(11b)   Some hints about the impact of emotion on perception come from research on the attentional-blink paradigm, research that shows people identify emotionally significant words faster than neutral words.

---

[3] By analogy, we can be grateful that the story of the three little pigs wasn't written like this: "The third little pig built a house of bricks, which he bought at the local home improvement center, although he could have paid less for the bricks online."

In 11b, the clause leads with *research*, so the reader avoids the ambiguity of *which*. In other words, the repeated noun (*research*) anchors the clause, telling readers where they're headed. In the process, it avoids a sprawling sentence that seems to have no direction.

Sentences 12a and 12b illustrate the shortcomings of introducing a clause with *which* and the benefits of replacing *which* with its antecedent.

> (12a)   Participants were asked to recall locations on a college campus, which were chosen to be particularly salient for undergraduates.

> (12b)   Participants were asked to recall locations on a college campus, locations that were chosen to be particularly salient for undergraduates.

In 12b, I replaced *which* with *locations*. With this change, the reader immediately knows the topic of the clause and the sentence no longer sprawls.

Sometimes the topic of the dependent clause is such that no single word from the main clause is the antecedent for *which*. In this case, we use a word or phrase to summarize the relevant part of the main clause.

> (13a)   Women who expect to encounter sexism are particularly attentive to words that are demeaning to females, which supports claims made by Allport (1954) more than 50 years ago.

In 13a, *which* introduces a clause that refers to the result described in the main clause; no noun from that clause can substitute for *which*. Instead, we can summarize that main clause by referring to it as *a result, a finding, an outcome*, or something similar:

> (13b)   Women who expect to encounter sexism are particularly attentive to words that are demeaning to females, a finding that supports claims made by Allport (1954) more than 50 years ago.

Replacing *which* with a specific noun or noun phrase reenergizes the sentence, giving it direction.

Sentences 14a and 14b provide another example:

> (14a)   When people feel grateful to another person, they are more likely to reciprocate a favor, which tends to strengthen interpersonal relationships.

EXERCISE 1.5

Reduce sentence sprawl by eliminating *which*.

1. Male infants are more likely than female infants to recognize a familiar stimulus in a novel orientation, which is consistent with research showing that males excel at spatial tasks.
2. We tested participants on counting span, operation span, and reading span tasks, which are used to estimate working memory capacity.
3. Compared with high school students of the 1970s, today's high school students believe themselves to be more intelligent, which is further evidence for a trend of greater self-esteem in today's high school students.
4. *Experiencing stress often leads depressed individuals to lose sleep, which can make them have difficulty concentrating.

In this case, *which* refers to reciprocating a favor; *a behavior* or *an action* could be inserted instead:

(14b)   When people feel grateful to another person, they are more likely to reciprocate a favor, a behavior that tends to strengthen inter-personal relationships.

Sentence sprawl can't be blamed entirely on clauses that begin with *which*. Sometimes sentences sprawl when authors make comparisons or include lists. Sentence 15a illustrates sprawl from a comparison:

(15a)   Studies with this paradigm typically find that people view mem-bers of their own group as friendly and kind but that out-group members are perceived to be hostile.

Sentence 16a shows sprawl from a list:

(16a)   Motor vehicle accidents are a leading cause of deaths among adolescents because adolescents often exceed speed limits, driving is often done in conjunction with drinking alcohol, and seat belts are used rarely.

A good way to reduce the kind of sprawl seen in sentences 15a and 16a is by creating parallel structure—by expressing all the elements in the sentence in the same way, using the same grammatical forms. In sentence 15a, for exam-ple, the comparisons are completely inconsistent:

- one comparison involves <u>active voice</u> (*people . . . view members of their own group*) and another involves **passive voice** (*out-group members are perceived*);

- one comparison describes the <u>target group</u> completely (*members of their own group*), but the other uses <u>a shorthand</u> (*out-group members*); and

- one comparison mentions <u>two traits</u> (*friendly, kind*), but the other mentions only <u>one</u> (*hostile*).

By expressing all these comparisons in the same terms, we get a sentence that isn't much shorter than 15a but avoids its sprawl:

(15b)   Studies with this paradigm typically find that people view in-group members as friendly and kind but that they perceive out-group members as hostile and stingy.

Sentence 15b is easier to read because the comparisons are expressed using parallel structure: The voice is <u>active, t</u>he groups are described with <u>shorthand</u>, and the number of <u>traits is the same</u>.

We could shorten it further by deleting *that they perceive*:

(15c)   Studies with this paradigm typically find that people view in-group members as friendly and kind but out-group members as hostile and stingy.

And if you were really pressed for space, just use one trait per group:

(15d)   Studies with this paradigm typically find that people view in-group members as friendly but out-group members as hostile.

We can use parallel structure to make sentence 16a flow better and be more concise. The trick with this sentence is to recast all of the properties (speeding, drinking, not wearing seatbelts) in terms of how teenagers drive:

(16b)   Motor vehicle accidents are a leading cause of deaths among adolescents because adolescents often drive too fast, while drunk, and without wearing seatbelts.

Sometimes sprawl resists all of the techniques I've mentioned in the past few pages. In that case, there's no shame in splitting a long, sprawling sentence into two shorter, crisper sentences.

(17a) Risk-taking behavior is often thought to be a stable, pervasive personality trait, but recent research suggests that it is specific to particular domains, such as sports, gambling, or investment, which explains why sky divers and bungee jumpers do not frequent casinos or play the stock market.

Replacing *which* with *a result that* reduces the sprawl but still leaves a mouthful:

(17b) Risk-taking behavior is often thought to be a stable, pervasive personality trait, but recent research suggests that it is specific to particular domains, such as sports, gambling, or investment, a result that explains why sky divers and bungee jumpers do not frequent casinos or play the stock market.

It's time to bite the bullet and split the sentence in two:

(17c) Risk-taking behavior is often thought to be a stable, pervasive personality trait, but recent research suggests that it is specific to particular domains, such as sports, gambling, or investment. This result explains why sky divers and bungee jumpers do not frequent casinos or play the stock market.

When you split a sentence in this manner, consider using a semicolon to link the two independent clauses, like this:

(17d) Risk-taking behavior is often thought to be a stable, pervasive personality trait, but recent research suggests that it is specific to particular domains, such as sports, gambling, or investment; this result explains why sky divers and bungee jumpers do not frequent casinos or play the stock market.

This is a subtle cue to the reader that the two independent clauses are linked.

EXERCISE 1.6

Reduce the sprawl in these sentences by rewriting in parallel structure or as two sentences.

1. Among PhD-level scientists, those with greater SAT scores have more publications in scientific journals, and SAT score is positively correlated with the number of patents awarded.

2. For individuals who have approach goals in relationships, the number of positive features in the relationship predicts satisfaction with the relationship; when people have avoidance goals, relationship satisfaction is correlated with the absence of negative features in the relationship.

3. Research on the psychological correlates of human longevity shows that people with greater IQ scores tend to live longer, that greater conscientiousness is associated positively with longevity, and that the correlation between frequency of illness in childhood and age at death is negative.

4. *The impact of people's actions on their perception is illustrated by the findings that people judge a hill to be steeper when wearing a heavy backpack and that the size of a paddle is correlated negatively with people's estimate of the speed of the ball that they use to hit with the paddle.

WRAP-UP

1. Eliminate nominalizations by revising sentences to put actors in the subject and their actions in the verb.

2. Get to the subject quickly (avoid long introductory clauses) and don't interrupt the flow of subject-verb-object.

3. Avoid sentence sprawl by replacing *which* with nouns or noun phrases and by describing comparisons and lists in parallel.

FOR PRACTICE

1. Search an article for nominalizations; replace the ones that you find.

2. Search for long introductory clauses; shorten or eliminate them.

3. Go on a "*which* hunt"—find clauses that begin with *which* and replace *which* with a noun or a noun phrase.

ANSWERS TO EXERCISES[4]

Exercise 1.1

(1b)   After a *return* from the site of physical *activity*, *consumption* of a sandwich, an apple, and a Diet Coke was accomplished by me.

---

[4] The sentences I include here and throughout the book are designed to illustrate *possible* answers. Please don't consider your answer "wrong" if it doesn't match mine word for word. Your sentence may be better than mine!

(2a) The *demonstration* of contextual *influence* on visual *perception* is the primary *contribution* of this *report*.

(3a) *Overestimation* of negative *reactions* to unpleasant outcomes is common because of *underestimation* of *adjustment* to those outcomes.

Exercise 1.2

1. nominalization = extraction; actor = people; action = extracting the gist of a scene

    People extract the gist of a scene in a fraction of a second.

2. nominalization = focus; actor = our research; action = focus

    Our research focused on counterfactual reasoning.

3. nominalization = disclosure; actor = East Asians; action = disclosing personal information

    East Asians disclose personal information to friends less often than Westerners do.

Exercise 1.3

1. Bilingual children have greater cognitive control than monolingual children because bilingual children have extensive experience selecting one language for production and inhibiting another. OR

    Compared with monolingual children, bilingual children have greater cognitive control because they have extensive experience selecting one language for production and inhibiting another.

2. During interracial interactions, white and black individuals experience anxiety but detect it only in members of their own race. OR

    Black and white individuals experience anxiety during interracial interactions but detect such anxiety only in members of their own race.

3. We cannot determine whether today's college students are more narcissistic than prior generations of students because studies have relied on different measures of narcissism and samples have varied in the percentage of females that were included.

Exercise 1.4

1. Via pathways in visual and motor cortex, the size and orientation of an object affect how people grasp it. OR

Pathways in visual and motor cortex convey information about the size and orientation of an object that affects how people grasp the object.

2. For a range of problems, unconscious thinking leads to better solutions. OR

   Unconscious thinking leads to better solutions for a range of problems.

3. Although people remember exact pitch inaccurately, they are quite skilled at remembering patterns of changes in pitches. OR

   People forget pitches, but they remember patterns of changes in pitches.

Exercise 1.5

1. Male infants are more likely than female infants to recognize a familiar stimulus in a novel orientation, a result consistent with research showing that males excel at spatial tasks. OR

   . . . novel orientation, a finding consistent with research showing . . .

2. We tested participants on counting span, operation span, and reading span tasks, tasks used to estimate working memory capacity.

3. Compared with high school students of the 1970s, today's high school students believe themselves to be more intelligent, an outcome that represents further evidence for a trend of greater self-esteem in today's high school students. OR

   . . . more intelligent, an observation that represents . . .

Exercise 1.6

1. Among PhD-level scientists, those with greater SAT scores have more publications in scientific journals and more patents. OR

   Among PhD-level scientists, greater SAT scores are correlated positively with more publications in scientific journals and more patents.

2. For individuals who have approach goals in relationships, the number of positive features in the relationship predicts satisfaction with the relationship; for individuals who have avoidance goals, the absence of negative features in the relationship predicts satisfaction. OR

   Relationship satisfaction is predicted by the number of positive features in the relationship for people who have approach goals but by the absence of negative features for people who have avoidance goals.

3. Research on the psychological correlates of human longevity shows that people who live longer tend to have greater IQ scores, to be more conscientious, and to have been ill less often during childhood. OR

    Research on human longevity shows that it tends to be correlated positively with IQ scores, with conscientiousness, and with good health during childhood.

2

Adding Emphasis

Often you may want to emphasize an element of a text, such as a critical idea, an essential part of a procedure, or a key result. Novice writers sometimes convey emphasis with italic or bold fonts, but that practice often reveals that the author isn't confident that words alone will carry the message. In this lesson we'll consider two more effective ways to convey emphasis: through word choice and sentence structure.

CONVEYING EMPHASIS THROUGH WORD CHOICE

You can emphasize elements of a text by the words you use. Consider these two sentences—identical except for the italicized words:

(1a) The finding that parents *often* report greater happiness and greater life satisfaction than nonparents *seems to support* the evolutionary claim that parenting satisfies basic human needs.

(1b) The finding that parents *consistently* report greater happiness and greater life satisfaction than nonparents *confirms* the evolutionary claim that parenting satisfies basic human needs.

The second sentence seems more emphatic. Why? First, writing that "parents consistently report" describes a stronger finding than "parents often report." The former implies nearly all parents report greater happiness and satisfaction, but the latter implies only some do. Second, writing that this finding "confirms" the evolutionary claim is a much bolder statement than writing that the results merely "seem to support" that claim.

Words such as *consistently* and *confirm* are **intensifiers**—they convey boldness, strength, and confidence. As in this example, adverbs are often used as intensifiers (*very, quite, certainly, always*) as are verbs (*show, confirm, establish*) and adjectives (*key, crucial, essential, major*). Intensifiers function like the volume control on an amplifier, producing a "louder" text designed to ensure a reader doesn't miss a critical point.

Sometimes you may want to achieve the opposite effect: Instead of being bold and confident, you may want to be tentative and cautious. **Hedges** serve this function; for example, sentence 1a includes one hedge, *often*. Like intensifiers, hedges come as adverbs (*often, sometimes*), adjectives (*many, some*), and verbs (*suggest, seems*).

Sentence 2a begins with a neutral statement, and sentences 2b and 2c show the impact of adding an intensifier and hedge, respectively.

(2a) Executive function predicts performance on analogical reasoning problems.

(2b) Executive function *invariably* predicts performance on analogical reasoning problems.

(2c) Executive function *occasionally* predicts performance on analogical reasoning problems.

Sentence 2b is bold, telling the reader that the link between executive function and analogical reasoning is ironclad. In contrast, sentence 2c is much softer, describing the link as weak or fleeting.

EXERCISE 2.1

Identify the hedges and intensifiers in these sentences.

1. Individuals who recognize emotions accurately tend to be more successful negotiators.
2. Unlike conservatives, liberals invariably view environmental issues in moral terms.
3. Critical influences on the ease with which children learn to read are letter-sound knowledge and phoneme awareness.
4. People typically judge threatening stimuli to be physically closer than they are.
5. *After being involved in an automobile accident, drivers often avoid taking risks.

EXERCISE 2.2

Revise these sentences twice, once by intensifying and once by hedging.

1. People's posture expresses how powerful they feel.
2. Because better educated people have greater knowledge of health-related behavior, they are healthier than less educated people.
3. Overhearing other people talk on cell phones is annoying because we hear only half of the conversation.
4. People who feel rejected and alienated are more aggressive verbally and physically.
5. *Adolescents who are members of one stigmatized group (e.g., African Americans) are intimidated by prejudice aimed at adolescents who are members of other stigmatized groups (e.g., females).

You should choose intensifiers and hedges carefully. Writing that's filled with intensifiers can seem arrogant, a tone many readers find offensive. The three sentences in paragraph 3a are filled with intensifiers:

(3a)   When people feel sad, they *invariably* think more deliberately. They have a *very* realistic view of their abilities and *never* rely on stereotypes. Consequently, these findings *affirm* the old saying that "sadder is wiser."

Instead of respecting a reader's ability to reflect on a passage and draw reasonable conclusions, authors who write like this seem to be saying to a reader, "Open wide because I'm about to force a conclusion down your throat." So, use intensifiers carefully.

But writing that's replete with hedges is also ineffective. Here's the previous paragraph, with a hedge replacing each intensifier.

(3b)   When people feel sad, they *sometimes* think more deliberately. They *may* have a realistic view of their abilities and *typically* do not rely on stereotypes. Consequently, these findings *appear to support* the old saying that "sadder is wiser."

Readers also react negatively to this version of the paragraph, but for different reasons. The reader thinks the author spineless—unwilling to state anything with confidence. And if the author lacks confidence in the writing, why should the reader trust the writing or, for that matter, even bother to read it?

These last two paragraphs underscore the need to balance hedging and intensifying, of finding a voice that is neither arrogant nor timid but instead cautiously confident. As you try to find this voice, one strategy is to start

EXERCISE 2.3

Revise each paragraph twice, once in a cautious voice and again in a bold (but *not* a shove-it-down-your-throat) voice.

1. In Experiment 1, participants were more likely to remember a friend's birthday when that birthday was close to the participant's. In Experiment 2, participants learned more about a hypothetical person when that person's birthday was close to the participant's. These findings indicate that people are better able to remember information that is relevant to them personally.

2. *Frequent switching between tasks has costs and benefits. On the one hand, task switching leads people to err more often because the demands of the prior task interfere with those of the current task. On the other hand, task switching causes people to be more creative because it induces them to approach a task from a new perspective.

with a draft that includes <u>no hedges or intensifiers</u>; if they are stripped from paragraph 3b, we get this:

> (3c)   When people feel sad, they think more deliberately. They have a realistic view of their abilities and don't rely on stereotypes. Consequently, these findings support the old saying that "sadder is wiser."

You'll notice that without hedges or intensifiers, the paragraph seems reasonably confident. That's usually true: The absence of hedges typically produces a text that's fairly strong. (Notice that in this last sentence, I hedged three times!) Intensifiers should be added with care because they may change the tone from confident to arrogant. However, adding a hedge or two is often useful because it signals the reader that you've got faith in what you're writing but appreciate that the arguments may not be bulletproof (e.g., a result may be open to another interpretation).

Finally, avoid combining hedges and intensifiers in a way that sends a mixed message to your reader. For example, if you hedge your findings, it's best not to intensify the conclusions you draw from those findings. Be particularly careful to avoid combining hedges and intensifiers in the same sentence (e.g., "these findings definitely suggest" or "the results seem to confirm") as this will definitely confuse your readers. Probably.

CONVEYING EMPHASIS THROUGH SENTENCE STRUCTURE

A politician giving a speech, a marathoner nearing the finish line, and a salesperson negotiating a deal have something in common: They want to end strong. This same strategy works for conveying emphasis in your writing. You want to conclude a sentence strongly, saving the important, innovative, or provocative points for the end. For example, suppose you wanted to describe the emergence of a new theoretical framework. You might write the following:

(4a)   A powerful theoretical framework for studying memory monitoring is suggested by these findings.

But you emphasize the theoretical framework by putting it at the end of the sentence:

(4b)   These findings suggest a powerful theoretical framework for studying memory monitoring.

Now consider this pair of sentences:

(5a)   Stable and substantial individual differences in working memory are shown in performance on N-back, complex span, and delayed matching-to-sample tasks.

(5b)   Based on performance on N-back, complex span, and delayed matching-to-sample tasks, individual differences in working memory are stable and substantial.

Sentence 5a puts working-memory tasks at the end, and this position of emphasis suggests that the author will be focusing on those tasks. In contrast, sentence 5b puts individual differences at the end, a change that leads the reader to expect more about the nature of those individual differences.

Let's look at some techniques for ending sentences with a bang, not a whimper.

Cut Unnecessary Material at the End of a Sentence

Consider this:

(6a)   Individuals who have near-death experiences often renew their appreciation for life, with all of its ups and downs.

EXERCISE 2.4

Trim unnecessary words to create greater emphasis.

1. When people are administered oxytocin, they are more cooperative with other people.
2. Among children who experience a natural disaster (e.g., Hurricane Katrina), those who view extensive TV coverage of the disaster often experience stress in their daily lives.
3. Multiple-choice tests do little to foster learning because the student need only recognize, not retrieve, the correct answer to the question.
4. *Parents must certify that they are eligible for subsidies by documenting their wages in person or online.

The important claim here is the link between near-death experiences and appreciation for life. Adding "with all of its ups and downs" contributes nothing because it simply mentions properties of life familiar to most readers. Eliminating that phrase puts the emphasis where it belongs, on renewed appreciation for life.

(6b)   Individuals who have near-death experiences often renew their appreciation for life.

Here's another example:

(7a)   When people are tired, their minds often wander from the task they are performing at the time.

This sentence is ineffective because the critical link—between fatigue and mind wandering—is obscured by the long description of the task. This is better:

(7b)   When people are tired, their minds often wander from the current task.

Put Context-Setting Material at the Beginning of a Sentence

Sometimes you may want to put a statement in context. For example, you might want to cite the source of findings that support a claim. Or you might want to indicate that a statement applies broadly, across cultures, domains, or conditions. Such context-setting remarks work better at the beginning of a sentence than at the end. Look at the following pair of sentences:

(8a)   Based on findings from the Add Health Study, individuals who have first sexual intercourse in early adolescence are more likely to be dissatisfied with their romantic relationships as adults.

(8b)   Individuals who have first sexual intercourse in early adolescence are more likely to be dissatisfied with their romantic relationships as adults, based on findings from the Add Health Study.

The interesting finding here is the link between timing of first sexual intercourse and satisfying romantic relationships during adulthood. Sentence 8a emphasizes that result by placing it at the end of the sentence. In contrast, sentence 8b starts with the interesting result but ends weakly by specifying the source of the data producing the result.

The next pair of sentences shows the same pattern:

(9a)   On many cognitive tasks, older adults respond more slowly than younger adults.

(9b)   Older adults respond more slowly than younger adults on many cognitive tasks.

Sentence 9a gets the information about tasks out of the way and finishes strong by emphasizing age-related differences in speed of response. In contrast, sentence 9b leads with that interesting result but then ends feebly by mentioning tasks where that result is observed.

There is an important exception to the rule of putting context-setting information at the beginning of a sentence: Sometimes information about context is to be emphasized, which means it should appear at the end of the sentence, not the beginning. For example, sentence 8b might be preferred over sentence 8a if the critical idea is that the link between adolescent sex and relationship satisfaction is based on a single study and should be replicated. Similarly, sentence 9b would work better than sentence 9a if the goal were to establish that age-related differences appear on most cognitive tasks, not just a few.

EXERCISE 2.5

Revise each sentence so that the context-setting material in italics appears at the beginning of the sentence.

1. Higher levels of the hormone oxytocin are associated with greater distress in interpersonal relationships, *but this relationship is found only for women.*
2. People's beliefs about the severity of a health problem influence whether they act to prevent that problem, *according to the health belief model.*
3. The physiological bases for excellence in distance running are well known, *although the psychological bases are not.*
4. *Conscientiousness predicted performance on jobs that allow workers to make their own decisions, as was true for emotionality.*

Move Important Elements Toward the End of the Sentence

Sometimes you want to move words toward the end of the sentence so they receive the emphasis they deserve. Here are two techniques to do this:

1. *Insert* there/it/what + *a verb (usually a form of* to be, *such as* is, are, was, *or* were):

Sentence 10a is clear but lacking in punch.

(10a) People more often cheat in a dimly lit room.

In 10a, the important ideas are distributed across the entire sentence: *People* is the subject's sentence, *cheat* is the verb, and the **prepositional phrase** *in a dimly lit room* ends the sentence. In contrast, 10b is strong because all these ideas are moved closer to the end of the sentence and united in an independent clause at the end of the sentence:

(10b) There is compelling evidence that people more often cheat in a dimly lit room.

Similarly, sentence 11a is clear but weak:

(11a) When humans look at a location where food is hidden, dogs look for the food in that spot.

But starting the sentence with "What is striking is that" puts the critical information closer to the end of the sentence:

(11b) What is striking is that when humans look at a location where food is hidden, dogs look for food in that spot.

Finally, sentence 12b uses "It is" to achieve greater emphasis:

(12a) Profiles on Facebook depict personality reasonably accurately.

(12b) It is noteworthy that profiles on Facebook depict personality reasonably accurately.

Use these techniques sparingly, saving them for sentences that demand emphasis. Why? First, these techniques contradict the advice, from Lesson 1, that sentences have strong subjects and strong verbs. "It is" and "there are" are hollow (one reason why some teachers and editors suggest writers avoid them altogether). Second, they make sentences longer, which goes against the goal of writing concisely. Nevertheless, used occasionally, these techniques help draw the reader's attention to a key point.

2. Add *not only X but Y.*

One way to create emphasis is to contrast one element with others. For example, perhaps X is known to affect performance on a task; your work shows that Y is an additional influence. The *not only X but Y* construction makes this comparison explicit and conveniently puts Y at the emphasis-receiving end of the sentence.

Suppose you've conducted a study on the impact of playing violent video games. You find that boys who play these games frequently are more aggressive and less engaged in school. The former result replicates previous studies, but the latter result is novel. You might write this:

(13a) Adolescent boys who spend more time playing violent video games are more aggressive and less engaged in school.

This sentence is clear but does not highlight the novel result. Using *not only X but Y* makes the novel result stand out:

(13b) Adolescent boys who spend more time playing violent video games are not only more aggressive but less engaged in school.

Similarly, if your novel claim is that ethical values influence consumer behavior, you might write this:

(14a) Consumers choose products based on price, quality, and a sense of social responsibility.

This is clear but does little to sell the novel idea.

(14b) Consumers choose products based not only on price and quality but on a sense of social responsibility.

Sentence 14b is more effective because *not only X but Y* contrasts the new idea with the accepted ideas.

Used effectively, *not only X but Y* is a powerful tool for highlighting new information. But many writers use it incorrectly, misplacing *only*. For *not only X but Y* to work, X and Y must be the same part of speech. For example, consider these sentences:

(15a) Children with siblings are not only gregarious but creative.

(15b) Children with siblings not only are gregarious but creative.

EXERCISE 2.6

Use the four techniques I've just described to revise each of these sentences so the material to be emphasized is moved closer to the end of the sentence.

1. Individuals differ consistently in the emotions they feel most frequently and in the emotions they typically elicit in other people.
2. People are at greater risk for suicide when they have attempted suicide previously and when they have implicit thoughts about death.
3. For dogs and people, glucose boosts self-control.
4. When choosing a potential mate, humans consider features that can be assessed quickly because they are visible (e.g., height, weight) as well as features that require more time and effort to assess (e.g., education, occupation).
5. *Attentional skill and bilingualism predict performance on tasks that measure executive function.

Sentence 15a is correct because X and Y are both adjectives (*gregarious, creative*). Sentence 15b is incorrect because X is a verb phrase (*are gregarious*) but Y is an adjective (*creative*).

Similarly, in this pair of sentences

(16a) People who are depressed not only are irritable but feel helpless.

(16b) People who are depressed are not only irritable but feel helpless.

Sentence 16a is correct because X and Y are both verb phrases (*are irritable, feel helpless*). Sentence 16b is incorrect because X is an adjective (*irritable*) but Y is a verb phrase (*feel helpless*). So, after you've written a sentence that includes *not only X but Y* be sure to check that X and Y belong to the same grammatical class.

WRAP-UP

1. Use intensifiers to add emphasis and hedges to convey caution. But don't overuse these words: Too many intensifiers make your writing seem arrogant, and too many hedges make it seem feeble.

2. Put material you want to emphasize at the end of the sentence. Techniques for doing this include eliminating unnecessary words, putting qualifying comments at the beginning of a sentence, and shifting text to the right.

FOR PRACTICE

1. Identify hedges and intensifiers in a randomly selected paragraph; replace hedges with intensifiers and vice versa.

2. Find sentences that include unnecessary material at the end, material that causes them to end weakly.

3. Find sentences that put qualifying material in an introductory clause. Rewrite the sentences to have this material at the end; notice how the emphasis changes.

4. Find sentences that use *that/it/what* for emphasis. Delete this material and note the change in emphasis.

5. Find sentences that list multiple elements; revise using *not only X but Y* to emphasize one element.

ANSWERS TO EXERCISES

Exercise 2.1

1. Individuals who recognize emotions accurately *tend* to be more successful negotiators. (hedge)

2. Unlike conservatives, liberals *invariably* view environmental issues in moral terms. (intensifier)

3. *Critical* influences on the ease with which children learn to read are letter-sound knowledge and phoneme awareness. (intensifier)

4. People *typically* judge threatening stimuli to be physically closer than they are. (hedge)

Exercise 2.2

1. People's posture *seems to* express how powerful they feel. (hedge with verb)

   People's posture *consistently* expresses how powerful they feel. (intensify with verb)

2. Because better educated people have greater knowledge of health-related behavior, they are *inevitably* healthier than less educated people. (intensify with adverb)

   Because better educated people have greater knowledge of health-related behavior, they are *typically* healthier than less educated people. (hedge with adverb)

3. Overhearing other people talk on cell phones is *often* annoying because we hear only half of the conversation. (hedge with adverb)

Overhearing other people talk on cell phones is *invariably* annoying because we hear only half of the conversation. (intensify with adverb)

4. *All* people who feel rejected and alienated are more aggressive verbally and physically. (intensify with adjective)

People who feel rejected and alienated *tend to be* more aggressive verbally and physically. (hedge with verb)

Exercise 2.3

Cautious version:

In Experiment 1, *most* participants were more likely to remember a friend's birthday when that birthday was close to the participant's. In Experiment 2, participants *sometimes* learned more about a hypothetical person when that person's birthday was close to the participant's. These findings *suggest* that people *tend to be* better able to remember information that is relevant to them personally.

(I added an adjective in the first sentence, an adverb in the second, and some verbs in the third.)

Bold version:

In Experiment 1, participants *usually* remembered a friend's birthday when that birthday was close to the participant's. In Experiment 2, participants learned more about a hypothetical person when that person's birthday was close to the participant's. These findings *indicate* that people *consistently* remember information that is relevant to them personally.

(In the first sentence, I replaced *were more likely to remember* with the stronger *usually*. In the second sentence, I dropped *usually* but didn't add an intensifier. In the last sentence, I added a stronger verb and a strong adverb.)

Exercise 2.4

1. When people are administered oxytocin, they are more cooperative ~~with other people~~. (By definition, cooperation involves other people.)

2. Among children who experience a natural disaster (e.g., Hurricane Katrina), those who view extensive TV coverage of the disaster often experience stress ~~in their daily lives~~. (Where besides daily living can stress affect a person?)

3. Multiple-choice tests do little to foster learning because the student need only recognize, not retrieve, the correct answer ~~to the question~~. (By definition, answers refer to questions.)

Exercise 2.5

1. For women, higher levels of the hormone oxytocin are associated with greater distress in interpersonal relationships.

2. According to the health belief model, people's beliefs about the severity of a health problem influence whether they act to prevent that problem.

3. Although psychological influences on distance running are unknown, the physiological bases for excellence in distance running are well known.

Exercise 2.6

1. It is striking that individuals differ consistently in the emotions they feel most frequently and in the emotions they typically elicit in other people. OR

   Individuals differ consistently not only in the emotions they feel most frequently but in the emotions they typically elicit in other people.

2. There is compelling evidence that people are at greater risk for suicide when they have attempted suicide previously and when they have implicit thoughts about death. OR

   It is noteworthy that people are at greater risk . . .

3. What emerges in this literature is that, for dogs and people, glucose boosts self-control. (To emphasize the similarity of the phenomenon across species, you could move the qualifying phrase to the end: What emerges in this literature is that glucose boosts self-control for dogs and people. Even better: What emerges in this literature is that glucose boosts self-control not only for people but for dogs.) OR

   There is abundant evidence that glucose boosts self-control in dogs and people.

4. When choosing a potential mate, humans consider not only features that can be assessed quickly because they are visible (e.g., height, weight) but features that require more time and effort to assess (e.g., education, occupation). OR

   What is noteworthy is that when humans choose a potential mate, they consider features that can be assessed quickly because they are visible (e.g., height, weight) as well as features that require more time and effort to assess (e.g., education, occupation).

3

Writing Concisely, With Some Spice

Confession time: This lesson is actually two mini-lessons, one about writing concisely and one about adding spice to your writing. Neither topic warrants a full lesson, so I've merged them here. We start with writing concisely.

WRITING CONCISELY

Scientific writing is concise. Why? One reason is that scientists are busy and can't waste time reading wordy reports. A second reason is that many journals limit the number of words they will allow in a manuscript. A third reason—my favorite—is that it's aesthetically satisfying to hit the "sweet spot" on length—just the right number of words for readers to understand a study fully, no more, no less.

In this half lesson, I mention four tips for concise writing.

Change Negatives to Affirmatives

Most phrases of the form *not* + *X* can be rewritten in the affirmative:

not missing ➝ present

not stop ➝ continue

not empty ➝ full

Sentence 1a includes such a *not* + *X* phrase:

(1a)   Salespeople more often invest extra effort when a customer is not rude.

If the *not* + *X* is replaced,

(1b)   Salespeople more often invest extra effort when a customer is polite.

we use one fewer word. Just as important, the sentence becomes slightly clearer because definitions involving the absence of features (e.g., *not rude*) are typically vaguer than those involving the presence of features (e.g., *polite*). In other words, definitions are more precise when they specify what something is rather than what it is not.

Delete What Readers Can Infer

Writers sometimes include adjectives that are redundant; they're unnecessary because they're implicit in the noun they modify. Examples include *terrible tragedy*, *true facts*, and *future plans*. By definition, tragedies are terrible, facts are true, and plans are for the future. The adjectives are wasted words. Consequently, in this sentence,

(2a)   After participants had completed the experiment, they were given a free gift.

we can delete *free* without any loss in meaning because by definition gifts are free:

(2b)   After participants had completed the experiment, they were given a gift.

EXERCISE 3.1

Change the negatives to affirmatives.

1.   There are not many studies on the impact of color on memory for scenes.
2.   People sometimes do not remember the source of their memories.
3.   Exposure to alcohol ads has behavioral consequences that do not differ from those obtained from actually consuming alcohol.
4.   *Manipulating task difficulty did not yield differences in mind wandering.

EXERCISE 3.2

Delete what readers can infer.

1. What's particularly striking is that the effect of misperception on intergroup conflict was large.
2. After participants had finished the perspective-taking task, they were tested on a working-memory task.
3. When people believe that free will is an illusion, they are more likely to behave in ways that are deceitful.
4. *After being ostracized by others, children reaffiliate with their own group.

Similarly, many adverbs are unnecessary because they're implicit in the verbs they modify. Examples here include *finish completely, prove conclusively*, and *suggest tentatively*.

A related mistake is to include categories that are implied by words. Examples include *period of time, red in color, triangular in shape, heavy in weight*, and *depreciate in value*. In each of these cases, the category (e.g., time, color, shape) is implied by the initial noun, adjective, or verb. In sentence 3a, for example,

(3a)   All the participants were of the male gender.

gender is unnecessary because it's implicit in male:

(3b)   All the participants were male.

This tip, like the previous one, saves only a word or two. But these can add up over the course of a manuscript.

Replace Phrases With Words

English is filled with short phrases that can be replaced with a single word. Table 2 lists some illustrative examples, but there are dozens more!

For example, in sentence 4a,

(4a)   In the event that synesthesia is a product of learning, pairing of sounds and visual symbols reflects a person's experiences.

"In the event that" can be replaced by *If*—saving three words (and 15 characters!).

TABLE 2   **Common Phrases That Can Be Replaced by a Single Word**

Phrase	Word
A large percentage of	Most
As a consequence of	Because
At that point in time	Then
At the present time	Now
Due to the fact that	Because
Has a requirement for	Needs
In a timely manner	Promptly
In close proximity to	Near
In some cases	Sometimes
In the near future	Soon
In the situation where	When
Subsequent to	After
With reference to	About
With the exception of	Except

(4b)   If synesthesia is a product of learning, pairing of sounds and visual symbols reflects a person's experiences.

Because English has so many phrases like those in Table 2, you can't hope to remember them all. Instead, as you edit your writing, pay attention to sets of words that gain their meaning from being together. Then see if you can replace them with a single word.

EXERCISE 3.3

Identify phrases that can be replaced by an individual word.

1. Participants were told to determine the location of the target in an array of photographs.
2. Emotionally significant words have a tendency to be identified more accurately than emotionally neutral words.
3. During the time that participants in the control group were sitting, those in the experimental group were jogging.
4. *When people experience awe, this has an effect on their humility.

Delete Adverbs and Adjectives

This may seem like a radical proposal—eliminating two parts of speech! However, too many writers insert adjectives or adverbs that have little meaning. Consequently, a good revision strategy is to create a version of a sentence with no adjectives or adverbs and then reinsert only those essential to the sentence's meaning.

In sentence 5a, the adjectives and adverbs are in italics; in sentence 5b, they've been deleted.

> (5a) Interviewers *often* gesture during *routine investigative* interviews, a *nonverbal* behavior that *certainly* affects the interviewee's *vocal* responses.

> (5b) Interviewers gesture during interviews, a behavior that affects the interviewee's responses.

One approach is to rank the deleted words in their importance to the sentence. (Of course, the surrounding sentences provide a context that determines the importance of individual words; not knowing that context, our choices are more tentative.) Of the six italicized words (*often, routine, investigative, nonverbal, certainly, vocal*), I would rank *investigative* as the most important; it seems essential because it identifies the setting in which gestures take place. I would rank *routine* and *certainly* as the least important. How does a routine investigative interview differ from one that's nonroutine? *Certainly* is an intensifier that's unnecessary: *behavior that affects the interviewee's responses* is sufficiently strong. *Often* is a hedge; it could be included if the authors want to be cautious regarding their claims. *Nonverbal* and *vocal* might help to emphasize the contrast between different modes of communicative behavior. My preferred version of the sentence is this:

> (5c) Interviewers *often* gesture during *investigative* interviews, a *nonverbal* behavior that *certainly* affects the interviewee's *vocal* responses.

Sentence 6a provides another example in which adjectives and adverbs are italicized; in sentence 6b, they've been omitted.

> (6a) Following a violation of *human* trust, a *sincere* apology repairs trust only when people *really* believe that *moral* character is *actually* malleable.

> (6b) Following a violation of trust, an apology repairs trust only when people believe that character is . . .

Of the six deleted words—*human, sincere, really, moral, actually, malleable*—two seem essential: *moral* and *malleable*. Both are at the heart of the story; apologies "work" when people believe a person's moral nature can be changed. But none of the rest seems essential: *trust* is usually between people, and the rest of the sentence makes it clear that this story is about human trust. Unless indicated to the contrary, apologies are assumed to be *sincere*, and *really* and *actually* add nothing (e.g., *is actually malleable* = *is malleable*). Sentence 6c is the version I prefer:

(6c) Following a violation of trust, an apology repairs trust only when people believe that *moral* character is *malleable*.

This delete-all-adjectives-and-adverbs strategy is labor intensive but worth the effort: In both examples, four words were deleted, producing sentences that were not only shorter but crisper. Until this leaner style of writing comes naturally, one step of your revising might be to delete one adjective (or adverb) from every sentence, or five from each paragraph. For some sentences and paragraphs this won't be possible. But most of the time you'll find plenty of excess adjectives and adverbs, a process that will hone your skill in identifying nonessential words. And used with the other strategies mentioned here (change negatives to affirmatives, delete what readers can infer, replace phrases with words), your writing will get closer to that aesthetically pleasing sweet spot on length.[1]

EXERCISE 3.4

Identify all the adjectives and adverbs; delete those that are unnecessary.

1. Married individuals who verbally report having a truly happy marriage actually have better physical health and increased longevity.
2. The testing effect refers to the psychological phenomenon that repeated retrieval of information actually helps people to remember that same information much better.
3. When people listen carefully to extremely sad music, they are relatively biased to hear many words related to death.
4. *Infants carefully evaluate unfair male and female adults very negatively but do not punish them.

---

[1] One common adverb to avoid is *very* because *very* + *adjective* typically can be replaced with a single adjective that's more precise. For example, replace *very smart* with *brilliant*, replace *very thin* with *emaciated*, and replace *very happy* with *euphoric*.

ADDING SPICE

I've searched the Internet high and low but can't find a single website that says scientific writing should be boring. Nevertheless, many writers seem to strive for a style that's clear but so dull that *How to Repair Your Lawnmower* seems riveting by comparison. This is silly; science is not well served when reading articles is tedious. Science is exciting, and there's no reason why articles shouldn't convey that excitement to the reader. In this mini-lesson, I suggest several tips for spicing up your scientific writing. They won't turn you into a bestselling novelist, but they will help to create a story line that's lively and engaging. What's more, many of these tips will help your readers to understand your work and remember your findings.

Writing Actively

In the lesson on writing clearly, I emphasized that sentences are easier to understand when they have actors as subjects and their actions as verbs. That practice also makes your writing more animated and more appealing. As a reminder of the pitfalls of sentences filled with nominalizations, sentence 7a

(7a)   Income inequality at the national level is negatively correlated with happiness.

is no more engaging than a repair manual. But revised to emphasize characters and actions,

(7b)   People are relatively happy when their country's wealth is distributed evenly.

the sentence comes alive; it's no longer about abstractions but what makes people happy.

Figures of Speech

Skilled writers often enrich their prose with figures of speech—devices in which words are used in special ways to achieve a distinct effect. For example, in **hyperbole**, exaggerated statements are used for emphasis. In **understatement**, the description is deliberately less strong than the facts or conditions warrant. Frankly, both hyperbole and understatement are risky for scientific writing because readers may interpret them literally, not figuratively.

Simile and Metaphor

Other figures of speech are more useful. Both's **Simile** and **metaphor** involve comparing dissimilar objects, typically so the text is clearer or more vivid.

In other words, similes and metaphors can aid comprehension by comparing a novel idea or concept with familiar ideas or concepts. For example, sentence 8 refers to the familiar Nike swoosh to indicate the reliable signs of ADHD.

(8)   Hyperactivity, inattention, and impulsivity signify ADHD, just as the swoosh signifies Nike products.

Similarly, sentence 9 uses grammar to introduce a system for combining goal-directed actions:

(9)   Just as grammar specifies legal combinations of words, means-end parse indicates how actions can be combined to achieve goals.

In addition to aiding comprehension, simile and metaphor can make sentences more vivid. They are often handy for emphasizing size-related phenomena, such as the strength of an effect, the likelihood an event will occur, or the (relative) ease of a task. Sentence 10 uses a simile to express how easily a target was detected:

(10)   The misoriented letter was detected as readily as a red cap on a field of new-fallen snow.

Sentence 11 uses a metaphor to emphasize that an effect was large:

(11)   The difference in change detection in the face and house conditions represents an industrial-strength effect.

Finally, sentence 12 uses a simile to emphasize that a phenomenon is likely:

(12)   In short, adolescents who are self-conscious in the presence of peers are as common as ants at a summer picnic.

Of course, metaphors and similes aren't restricted to size-related comparisons; most ideas can be made more familiar and more interesting with simile and metaphor. You can find scores of websites devoted to metaphors and similes that can inspire you to create your own. As you do, however, be wary of three traps that can snare a novice metaphor writer. (Notice that metaphor?) First, avoid mixed metaphors like the one in sentence 13a.

(13a)   Readers were flying high with congruous text but drowning with incongruous text.

The problem is that the sentence begins with a comparison to flying and then shifts to a comparison with swimming. Sentence 13b eliminates this problem by having a constant reference: smooth and difficult sailing.

> (13b)   Readers had smooth sailing with congruous text but encountered choppy water with incongruous text.

However, sentence 13b illustrates a second trap: a cliché. Hundreds (thousands?) of writers have used this comparison (smooth vs. choppy waters) before, which makes it less vivid. Sentence 14a has the same problem:

> (14a)   When walking on unsteady surfaces, infants are slower than snails.

Sentence 14b avoids the clichéd comparison:

> (14b)   When walking on unsteady surfaces, infants are slower than a checkout line at Best Buy on Black Friday.

Nevertheless, sentence 14b illustrates a third trap: Similes and metaphors are effective only when readers understand the reference—in this case, that a checkout line at Best Buy on Black Friday often moves very, very slowly. Readers who aren't familiar with Black Friday[2] (or don't know that Best Buy is a chain of electronics stores) will end up confused, not enlightened.

These examples show that the road to a successful metaphor is filled with obstacles. But creating an effective metaphor is worth the work because it animates your writing and makes it stand out from ordinary scientific text.

Antimetabole

You may not know another useful figure of speech by name, but you'll recognize familiar examples, all from U.S. presidents:

> (15)   What counts isn't necessarily the size of the *dog* in the *fight*—it's the size of the *fight* in the *dog*. (Eisenhower)

> (16)   Ask not what *your country* can do for *you*; ask what *you* can do for *your country*. (Kennedy)

---

[2] Black Friday is the Friday after the American Thanksgiving holiday and marks the start of the Christmas shopping season in the United States. Stores are usually packed with shoppers looking for good deals.

EXERCISE 3.5

Complete the sentence with a simile or metaphor. The words in brackets hint at a basis of comparison.

1. Speed of information processing increases steadily in childhood and adolescence, as if . . . [upgrading a computer's CPU].
2. When individuals with Parkinson's disease reach for an object, their hand moves a short distance, slows, and then moves again in a different direction like . . . [novice ship navigator].
3. According to ego-depletion theories, self-control depends on a limited pool of mental resources, just as . . . [muscle movements].
4. *Negative emotions such as anger are often tenacious, like . . . [an unwanted houseguest].

(17)   *America* did not invent *human rights* . . . *human rights* invented *America*. (Carter)

These examples illustrate **antimetabole**, a figure of speech in which words are repeated, in reverse order. Sentences 15 through 17 illustrate two main properties of antimetabole:

- The repeated words are often nouns or noun phrases.

- The nouns are usually linked by the same word (or words) in both instances.

A first step in creating your own antimetabole is to identify two nouns that refer to key elements in your work. Then think about verbs or phrases that describe how these elements are related in your work. As an example, consider research on people's religious beliefs. This work demonstrates wide-ranging behavioral consequences of belief in God but has done little to clarify the nature of those beliefs. I chose *God* and *belief* as the key nouns and after some experimentation came up with this:

(18)   Thus, research reveals much about the impact of *people's belief in God* but tells little about the *God in people's beliefs*.

As another example, sentence 19 summarizes findings that show mutual influence of emotional control on the quality of marriage:

(19)   Couples who frequently *control their emotions for the sake of their marriage* sometimes end up *controlling their marriage for the sake of their emotions*.

EXERCISE 3.6

Finish the sentence with an antimetabole that uses the italicized words and describes the findings in brackets.

1. *Neglecting your siblings* will lead . . . [siblings will ignore you].
2. When teams *lose sight of outcomes,* the likely . . . [they probably won't win].
3. People do not *know* how much others *remember* but . . . [other people's knowledge is something they do retain].
4. *If *leaders* emphasize a group's shared *values*, typically . . . [group members think highly of the people in charge of the group].

Creating good antimetaboles is challenging, but they can be remarkably effective, especially as the last sentence of a paper. It's not a coincidence that sentences with antimetabole rank high among the best-known quotations of historical figures.

Creating New Words

Many fiction writers create new words specifically to enliven their storytelling. Shakespeare was an expert, creating more than 1,000 new words (and we can thank him for the always useful *puke*), and modern novelists such as J. K. Rowling continue the practice (Plotnik, 2007). Used sparingly and carefully, such neologisms can enhance scientific writing.

There are many techniques for creating new words, including shortening an existing word (e.g., *prob* for *probably*, *obv* for *obviously*), blending existing words (e.g., *snowmageddon* to refer to a massive snowstorm, *Brangelina* to refer to Brad Pitt and Angelina Jolie), and using the names of well-known people as nouns or verbs (e.g., *Tebowing* to mean dropping to a knee to pray). Here I focus on three other options because they seem the easiest to use and work well with psychological content.

Adding Prefixes and Suffixes

English is filled with prefixes and suffixes; Table 3 lists some familiar examples. Adding one of them to an existing word is the simplest way to create a new word. For example, a meaning that is readily conveyed by gesture is *gesturable*; individuals who thrive on excluding others from social interactions are *excludaholics*.

Hyperhyphenated Modifiers

English is filled with hyphenated phrases that work as a unit to modify a word, typically a noun. Familiar examples include a *deer-in-the-headlights*

TABLE 3   **Common Prefixes and Suffixes That Can Be Used to Create New Words**

Prefix	Meaning	Suffix	Meaning
a (an)-	without	-able	capable of
macro/micro-	large/small	-aholic	one addicted to something
mis-	faulty	-cian/-ee/-er	one who
neo-	new	-ism	belief system
omni-	all, always	-ize	to cause
pseudo-	fake, false	-ness	state of

EXERCISE 3.7

Combine the italicized word with a prefix or suffix from Table 3 to make a new word that fits the definition given in each sentence.

1. A facial expression that looks like a *smile* but isn't because it doesn't engage muscles in the mouth and eyes.
2. A pattern of *transfer* in which original learning extends to nearly all novel tasks.
3. People who *plan* compulsively.
4. **Optimism* that is not warranted.

look, a *state-of-the-art* computer, and an *over-the-top* experience. But you can create your own hyphenated phrases, as I did on page 20 in suggesting that you avoid a *shove-it-down-your-throat* voice. Some other examples include *choke-under-pressure* leaders, *aggressive-toward-other-people* dreams, and *faster-reaction-times-are-associated-with-reduced-mortality* effects.

A common situation where hyperhyphenation is useful is a sentence with a long noun phrase, such as sentence 20a:

(20a)   The finding that memory was superior for the location of taboo words supports . . .

This sentence is difficult because readers must slog through a long phrase before they get to the main verb: 10 words separate the subject, *finding*, from the verb, *supports*. Using hyperhyphenation produces this:

(20b)   The superior-memory-for-location-of-taboo-words finding supports . . .

Hyperhyphenation cues the reader that the words should be a unit. Placing them before the noun (as with any adjective) puts the subject and verb of the sentence together. But the main reason for hyperhyphenation is that its very

EXERCISE 3.8

Hyperhyphenate to create a phrase that modifies the italicized noun.

1. The *motive* to perceive the social system as fair is particularly well established . . .
2. The findings help to explain the prevalence of *people* who see the forest before the trees.
3. *People* performing better in the morning illustrates . . .
4. *In free recall tasks, the *strategy* to begin by recalling the items presented last . . .

novelty (particularly in scientific writing) highlights the hyphenated words and, in the process, adds some zip to your text.

Before you go wild with hyperhyphenation, some warnings. First, don't use a hyperhyphenated phrase when an existing adjective would fit perfectly. If you write *have-abundant-material-possessions people* instead of *affluent people*, readers will think that either your vocabulary is limited or you're showing off. Second, be particularly careful when using hyperhyphenated phrases to describe people because this can be dehumanizing (i.e., it equates the person with the description and makes the person nothing more than a group member). In other words, people with many material possessions are not just wealthy; they may also be friendly, happy, or irresponsible. Referring to them as *affluent people* reduces them to a single dimension and makes the group seem more homogeneous than it is. Third, avoid *Hey!-look-what-I-can-do-with-lots-of-hyphens-in-my-writing-to-get-your-undivided-attention* phrases. As a rule of thumb, hyperhyphenated phrases are probably most effective when they include three to five words.

Verbing

Fifty years ago, *dialogue*, *impact*, and *message* were used only as nouns, but today each is often used as a verb.

(21)   Effective bosses frequently *dialogue* with their employees.

(22)   Learning a second language during childhood can *impact* the development of executive control.

(23)   Western adolescents often *message* their feelings rather than showing them overtly.

Such verbing is most effective when the meaning of the new verb is novel and obvious. The well-known *google* fits these criteria. So does *podium*, as in *The relay team hopes to podium in the upcoming Olympic games.*

To do your own verbing, search for nouns. You'll discover that many don't qualify because they already have verb forms. (Remember, this is how nominalizations are created, by making a noun from a verb or adjective.) Good candidates are often nouns that serve as objects of verbs. For example, in sentence 24a

>   (24a)   Strangers often achieve *rapport* when their body movements are coordinated.

rapport is the object of achieve. In sentence 24b, it's a new verb:

>   (24b)   Strangers often *rapport* when their body movements are coordinated.

Similarly, in sentence 25a

>   (25a)   Pursuing a *goal* often happens unconsciously.

goal is the object of pursuing. In sentence 25b, it's become a verb:

>   (25b)   *Goaling* often happens unconsciously.

As you pursue verbing, two words of caution. First, be sure that the new verb captures the meaning of the words it's replacing. For example, in my first attempts to write this section, I thought *gist* was a good candidate for verbing, as shown in the following pair of sentences:

>   (26a)   Adults readily recall the *gist* of stories.

>   (26b)   Adults *gist* stories.

In fact, *gist* didn't work well as a verb because *gist stories* does not necessarily imply *recall the gist of stories*. It might mean that adults readily perceive the gist of stories or refer to other actions people might perform on *gist*.

Second, as was true for words created from prefixes and suffixes, verbed words are best used after the context establishes their meaning, such as at the end of an Introduction or Discussion section. And I recommend you create no more than one or two new words per paper. With one (or two) new words, readers are likely to enjoy the novelty and appreciate the descriptive power of the new word. With more than two new words, readers will find you guilty of way-over-the-top writing.

EXERCISE 3.9

Enliven these sentences by making the italicized word a verb.

1. Parents are rarely successful when they try to make their shy children more *extroverted*.
2. Contact with *nature* makes people feel happy.
3. People who violate *taboos* (e.g., they cheat or steal) often are punished for their behavior.
4. *Choosing between inexpensive and environmentally friendly products often is a *quandary* for consumers.

WRAP-UP

1. Make your writing more concise by changing negatives to affirmatives, deleting what readers can infer, replacing phrases with words, and including only essential adjectives and adverbs.

2. Make your writing livelier by writing actively, relying on figures of speech (simile, metaphor, antimetabole), and creating new words.

FOR PRACTICE

1. Search for negatives and replace with affirmatives, replace phrases with words, and decide which adjectives and adverbs are unnecessary.

2. In an Introduction or Discussion section, clarify a complex idea with a simile or metaphor.

3. In the last paragraph of a Discussion, create a final sentence that includes antimetabole.

4. In an Introduction or Discussion section, create new words by adding a prefix or suffix, using hyperhyphenation or verbing.

ANSWERS TO EXERCISES

Exercise 3.1

1. There are *few* studies on the impact of color on memory for scenes.

2. People sometimes *forget* the source of their memories.

3. Exposure to alcohol ads has behavioral consequences that are *similar to* those obtained from actually consuming alcohol.

Exercise 3.2

1. What's particularly striking is that the effect of misperception on intergroup conflict was large ~~in size~~.

2. After participants had ~~completely~~ finished the perspective-taking task, they were tested on a working-memory task.

3. When people believe that free will is an illusion, they are more likely to behave in ways that are deceitful ~~in nature~~.

Exercise 3.3

1. Participants were told to ~~determine the location of~~ *find* the target in an array of photographs.

2. Emotionally significant words ~~have a tendency~~ *tend* to be identified more accurately than emotionally neutral words.

3. ~~During the time that~~ *While* participants in the control group were sitting, those in the experimental group were jogging.

Exercise 3.4

Adjectives and adverbs are in italics.

1. *Married* individuals who *verbally* report having a *truly happy* marriage *actually* have *better physical* health and *increased* longevity.

   Individuals who report having a *happy* marriage have *better physical* health and *increased* longevity. (Even better: Happily married individuals are healthier physically and live longer.)

2. The *testing* effect refers to the *psychological* phenomenon that *repeated* retrieval of information *actually* helps people to remember that *same* information *much* better.

   The *testing* effect refers to the phenomenon that *repeated* retrieval of information helps people to remember that information better.

3. When people listen *carefully* to *extremely sad* music, they are *relatively* biased to hear *many* words related to death.

   When people listen to *sad* music, they are biased to hear words related to death.

Exercise 3.5

1. Speed of information processing increases steadily in childhood and adolescence, as if the child's mental hardware is constantly being upgraded to a newer, faster CPU.

2. When individuals with Parkinson's disease reach for an object, their hand moves a short distance, slows, and then moves again in a different direction like a ship directed by an unskilled navigator.

3. According to ego-depletion theories, self-control depends on a limited pool of mental resources, just as movements of muscles draw from a limited supply of glucose.

Exercise 3.6

1. Neglecting your siblings will lead your siblings to neglect you.

2. When teams lose sight of outcomes, the likely outcome is to lose.

3. People do not know how much others remember, but they do remember how much others know.

Exercise 3.7

1. pseudosmile

2. omnitransfer

3. planaholics

Exercise 3.8

1. The *perceive-the-social-system-as-fair* motive is particularly well established . . .

2. The findings help to explain the prevalence of *see-the-forest-before-the-trees* people.

3. *Performing-better-in-the-morning* people illustrate . . .

Exercise 3.9

1. Parents are rarely successful when they try to *extrovert* their shy children.

2. *Naturing* makes people feel happy.

3. People who *taboo* (e.g., they cheat or steal) often are punished for their behavior.

4

The Art of Fine Paragraphs

If your sentences are clean, compelling, and lively, you're well on the way to joining the A-list of authors in psychology. But just as buying the best ingredients doesn't guarantee you'll prepare a gourmet meal, outstanding sentences alone won't guarantee an outstanding manuscript. You need to be able to assemble those excellent sentences into a coherent paragraph, a process we examine in this lesson. We'll start by examining the structure of paragraphs, then consider their flow and length.

STRUCTURE

A paragraph includes several sentences about one main idea. Not two, three, or four main ideas—just one. If you find yourself drifting to a new idea, start a new paragraph. That idea is normally expressed in the first sentence, called the **topic sentence**. Because it introduces the central idea of the paragraph, the topic sentence is crucial. It's followed by supporting sentences that develop the idea introduced in the topic sentence. A paragraph sometimes ends with a closing statement that restates the main idea and summarizes the supporting information.

The Topic Sentence

A strong topic sentence includes two parts: a topic and a controlling idea that specifies what the paragraph will say about the topic. In sentence 1, for example,

> (1)   The sex hormone testosterone has been linked to greater spatial ability in females.

the topic is testosterone, and the controlling idea is that testosterone is linked to greater spatial ability for females. Thus, the topic sentence gives the reader a road map for the rest of the paragraph—it will focus on the impact of testosterone on females' spatial ability. Similarly, in sentence 2,

> (2)   Following another person's gaze is a critical part of effective social interaction.

the topic is gaze following, and the controlling idea is the importance of gaze following for social interactions.

Well-written topic sentences are worth the effort because readers sometimes skim an article by reading only topic sentences. Consequently, topic sentences need to identify each step in the argument you develop, particularly in the Introduction and Discussion sections (there's more on this idea in Lessons 5 and 7).

Paragraph Development

A topic sentence is followed by three to six sentences that elaborate the controlling idea. That elaboration usually takes one of three forms in psychological

EXERCISE 4.1

Identify the topics and controlling ideas in these sentences.

1. Portion size influences how much food people eat.
2. Helping individuals orient to an environment and serving as markers for object locations are two proposed roles for landmarks.
3. Children who experience lower-quality maternal care respond less adaptively to stress.
4. *Typical-looking faces are judged to be more trustworthy.

writing. A common format is to elaborate by providing supporting details. Sentence 1, for example, might be elaborated by describing three to four examples illustrating a connection between testosterone and spatial ability:

(3)   For example, women who have more testosterone in saliva typically have greater spatial ability scores. In addition, women using oral contraceptives that contain progestin derived from testosterone respond faster on mental rotation problems. Finally, women exposed to atypically large amounts of testosterone during prenatal development respond more accurately on mental rotation tasks.

Each of these sentences illustrates a connection between testosterone and spatial ability.

In a second common format, the controlling idea involves competing theories or alternative hypotheses. Sentence 4a illustrates this type of topic sentence:

(4a)   The parental investment model predicts that jealousy takes different forms in males and female.

In the rest of the paragraph, the contrasting theories or hypotheses are described. With sentence 4a, this involves contrasting different forms of jealousy in males and females:

(4b)   The parental investment model predicts that jealousy takes different forms in males and females. On the one hand, males are more concerned about sexual infidelity because it increases the possibility that they may invest resources in offspring they have not fathered. On the other hand, females are more concerned about emotional infidelity because it increases the possibility that the father will abandon the mother and her offspring, depriving them of resources needed for child-rearing.

This kind of paragraph is often crucial in developing arguments in a manuscript, and consequently it's essential that it be written well. One formula for such a paragraph is to begin with a topic sentence that mentions alternative theories, hypotheses, explanations, or patterns of evidence. This is followed by *On the one hand* and a description of the first theory. Next comes *On the other hand* with a description of the second theory. Paragraph 5 illustrates this approach:

(5)   Scientists have proposed two competing views of personality disorders. *On the one hand*, they may represent a distinct clinical

syndrome that differs qualitatively from typical personality function. *On the other hand*, they may represent extreme variations of typical personality function that are maladaptive.

On the one hand and *on the other hand* make a great tool for showing readers the beginning and end of each description.[1]

This sort of paragraph is most effective when readers can easily see how the alternatives are similar and how they differ. These similarities and differences are most evident when the alternatives are described with sentences that rely on the same pattern of words, a technique known as parallel structure. To do this, try this trick: Describe the first alternative, then copy and paste your description and edit it as necessary so that it applies to the second alternative. Paragraph 6a has the topic sentence and a description of the first alternative, in this case, the pros and cons of taking notes in class with a computer.

(6a)   Educators debate the merits of taking notes in class in longhand or with a computer. On the one hand, taking notes with a computer is faster and more complete, but the notes are often verbatim and thus do not enhance learning.

The description of the second account begins by copying and pasting the first description, then, as necessary, replacing words from the first description. In sentence 7, deleted words have been crossed out and new words are in italics.

(7)   On the ~~one~~ *other* hand, taking notes ~~with a computer~~ *longhand* is ~~faster~~ *slower* and ~~more~~ *less* complete, but the notes are often ~~verbatim~~ *in a student's own words* and thus ~~do not~~ enhance learning.

Added to the first two sentences, the result is paragraph 6b:

(6b)   Educators debate the merits of taking notes in class in longhand or with a computer. On the one hand, taking notes with a computer is faster and more complete, but the notes are often verbatim and thus do not enhance learning. On the other hand, taking notes longhand is slower and less complete, but the notes are often in a student's own words and thus enhance learning.

---

[1] Never use *On the other hand* alone; always pair it with *On the one hand.* When you use *On the other hand* alone, many readers will assume they missed *On the one hand* and go backward through the manuscript trying to find it.

EXERCISE 4.2

Unscramble the sentences and then identify the type of development used in each paragraph.

1. In contrast, state anxiety is linked to characteristics of specific situations and consequently should affect attention through bottom-up processing. Trait anxiety is a by-product of an individual's personality and thus should affect attention through top-down processing. Trait and state anxiety affect attention through different mechanisms.
2. In other words, darkness makes people feel anonymous. Consequently, in darkness people are more often dishonest and selfish. According to this model, experiencing darkness leads people to believe they are relatively invisible.
3. The simplest is the number of lives saved. In health research, one of three measures is used to evaluate the life-saving impact of treatments. A third is the number of high-quality life years gained. Another is the number of life years gained.
4. *In turn, when children decode words easily and accurately, they better understand what they read. A common path to literacy starts with oral language skills. Children whose spoken language includes many words and complex grammar decode words more effectively.

The reader can easily compare the two modes of note taking because the sentences describing them have the same structure.

The last common type of paragraph describes processes that unfold over time. These paragraphs often describe sequences of behavior, series of cognitive processes, or steps in an experimental method. Paragraph 8 illustrates this structure:

(8)   Experimental trials involved four events. First, a fixation circle appeared at the center of the screen for 500 ms. Then the stimulus array appeared for 100 ms and was followed by a masking stimulus for 300 ms. Finally, participants reported the orientation of the target in the stimulus array.

This paragraph describes the order in which four events took place on each trial in an experiment.

Concluding Sentence

Most descriptions of paragraph structure include a concluding sentence that summarizes the paragraph's main points. However, for scientific writing, these are more appropriate for some paragraphs than others. For a paragraph that lists supporting information, a concluding sentence might refer to each of the cited points. For example, the italicized sentence summarizes the paragraph from passage 3:

(9)   The sex hormone testosterone has been linked to greater spatial ability in females. For example, women who have more testosterone in saliva typically have greater spatial ability scores. In addition, women using oral contraceptives that contain progestin derived from testosterone respond faster on mental rotation problems. Finally, women exposed to atypically large amounts of testosterone in prenatal development respond more accurately on mental rotation tasks. *Thus, greater levels of testosterone— reflecting individual differences, use of oral contraceptives, or prenatal exposure—are correlated with greater spatial skill.*

As in passage 9, concluding sentences are often marked by words that signal a conclusion, such as *thus, in summary,* or *to conclude.*

In paragraphs that contrast theories or hypotheses, a summary sentence should briefly cite each of the alternatives:

(10)   The parental investment model predicts that jealousy takes different forms in males and females. On the one hand, males are more concerned about sexual infidelity because it increases the possibility that they may invest resources in offspring they have not fathered. On the other hand, females are more concerned about emotional infidelity because it increases the possibility that the father will abandon the mother and her offspring, depriving them of resources needed for child-rearing. *In summary, according to the parental investment model, men's jealousy is rooted in sex, but women's jealousy is rooted in emotions.*

Notice that in this concluding sentence, the two alternatives are described in parallel structure, using the copy-and-paste technique described earlier:

(11)   In summary . . . men's jealousy is rooted in sex, but ~~men's~~ *women's* jealousy is rooted in ~~sex~~ *emotions.*

For these two kinds of paragraphs (i.e., those providing supporting information and those contrasting alternatives), a concluding sentence is most useful when the paragraphs are relatively long. In this case, readers often benefit from a reminder of the controlling idea and the evidence supporting it. And a concluding sentence provides a good sense of closure when the paragraph is at the end of the Introduction or Discussion sections. But for paragraphs that

EXERCISE 4.3

Add a concluding sentence to each of the paragraphs in Exercise 4.2.

include only three or four relatively simple sentences, concluding sentences are optional.

For the third common type of paragraph structure—that devoted to describing processes—concluding sentences are less common. This is particularly true for paragraphs describing experimental methods; concluding sentences are unnecessary. For paragraphs that describe behaviors or processes unfolding over time, a concluding sentence might simply list the first and last steps, perhaps with an illustrative intermediate step.

FLOW

A well-defined structure is an essential element of an effective paragraph. However, just as important are two other features: a seamless transition from one sentence to the next and a common perspective across all sentences in the paragraph.

Sentence Transitions

Readers enjoy paragraphs where sentences flow smoothly from one to the next, where ideas of the current sentence seem to emerge naturally from those expressed in prior sentences. To illustrate, compare passages 12a and 12b, in which the topic sentence is the same but the second sentence differs.

(12a) Clinical psychologists have searched for variables that would identify people at risk for suicide. Biological markers such as genotypes as well as behavioral markers such as suicidal thoughts have been studied by scientists.

(12b) Clinical psychologists have searched for variables that would identify people at risk for suicide. They have studied biological markers such as genotypes as well as behavioral markers such as suicidal thoughts.

Most readers find passage 12b is easier to read than passage 12a.

Similarly, compare passages 13a and 13b, which differ only in the second sentence.

(13a) People make inferences about other people from their facial expressions. They often use facial expressions to draw inferences about personality, health, and mood.

(13b) People make inferences about other people from their facial expressions. Personality, health, and mood are some of the domains in which they draw inferences from facial expressions.

Most readers believe that 13a is the easier passage; this passage seems to have better flow than passage 13b. Why? In passages 13a and 12b, the second sentence begins with information presented in the first sentence and then introduces new information. In passage 12b, the first sentence establishes that clinical psychologists have searched for predictors of suicidal behavior. In the second sentence, the subject and verb—*They have studied*—refer to the search mentioned in the first sentence. Then the new material—biological and behavioral markers—appears, after its meaning has been well established; biological and behavioral markers are what the psychologists mentioned in the first sentence have studied. In contrast, in passage 12a, the second sentence begins with the new information about specific markers, but their meaning isn't clear until the last five words of that sentence: *have been studied by scientists.*

This general principle—begin a sentence with familiar information and then introduce new information—explains why passage 13a is easier to read than passage 13b. In both passages, the first sentence establishes that people draw inferences from facial expressions. In passage 13a, the second sentence begins with this idea (*They often use facial expressions*) and then introduces specific domains in which people draw inferences. In contrast, the second sentence in passage 13b leads with new information about specific domains, and its significance isn't clear until the last half of the sentence.

Thus, starting sentences with familiar information establishes a context for new information and creates the sense of flow readers love. In other words, new ideas seem to appear seamlessly when they are firmly grounded in what the reader has read already. And there's an added benefit: Leading with familiar information puts the new information at the end of the sentence, prime territory for emphasizing new information (as described on pages 21–26).

The familiar→new principle also explains why those bad boys in the writing 'hood—nominalizations and passive voice—are valuable. Each can be used to begin a sentence with familiar information.

(14) Scientists have used rhythm to classify languages into those that are stress timed, syllable timed, and mora timed. This

classification helps to explain how infants exposed to two languages learn to distinguish those languages.

In passage 14, *classification* is a handy nominalization because it encapsulates the meaning of the first sentence and allows the second sentence to begin with familiar information.

Passive voice also allows you to start sentences with familiar information. In passage 15a,

> (15a) "Scary smart" individuals often make substantial contributions to literature, science, and the arts. Scores on intelligence and achievement tests identify such "scary smart" individuals, sometimes by early adolescence.

the second sentence begins with new information about test scores. In contrast, in passage 15b,

> (15b) "Scary smart" individuals often make substantial contributions to literature, science, and the arts. These individuals are often identified by early adolescence, using scores on intelligence and achievement tests.

the second sentence relies on passive voice to lead with familiar information (*These individuals are often identified . . .*).

EXERCISE 4.4

Revise the second sentence in each passage to improve flow.

1. When people read, they fixate briefly on a word and then move on to the next word. Less skilled readers tend to fixate on words longer than skilled readers do.
2. People who believe they are vulnerable to disease rely on heuristics to minimize their risks. Seeing themselves as more introverted (i.e., needing less social stimulation) and moving away from stimuli suggesting the presence of disease are typical heuristics.
3. If there are domain-general resources, then performance on verbal tasks should be impaired when people perform a visual-spatial task simultaneously. Studies of Austrian, Belgian, and German undergraduates have reported this outcome.
4. *Members of stigmatized groups often use strategies to create favorable impressions with other people. When other people seem to be stereotyping them, stigmatized individuals implement these strategies.

Nominalizations and passive voice are useful to begin sentences with familiar information, but you shouldn't take that as an invitation to use them all the time. Nominalizations and passive voice are not recommended for good storytelling because they make it harder to identify characters and their actions. However, in this case, that loss is balanced by enhancing flow across sentences. And this serves as a reminder that the recommendations made here are rules of thumb that sometimes conflict.

Finally, by design, some paragraphs have sentences that do not flow directly from one to the next. For example, when describing sequences of events, successive steps may have different contents, making it difficult to begin following sentences with familiar information. Passage 16a (a revised version of passage 8) illustrates this problem:

> (16a) Experimental trials involved four events. A fixation circle appeared at the center of the screen for 500 ms. The stimulus array

EXERCISE 4.5

Add transition words to help improve the flow of the paragraphs by making their organization more apparent.

1. The experiment included several phases linked by a cover story that the experiment concerned taste preferences. The participant was seated with two confederates and asked to complete questionnaires concerning mood and taste preferences. While waiting for the experimenter to return, one confederate took a toy from a shelf and began throwing it to others; the participant received 5% of the throws in the ostracized condition but 33% in the included condition. The participant was asked to choose a type of hot sauce for a stranger; choices were labeled *mild*, *medium*, and *hot*.

2. According to life history theory, individuals differ in how they allocate resources to offspring. In a "fast" strategy, more offspring are produced, but parents invest relatively less time and energy in their offspring. This strategy is more common when the environment is harsh, such that offspring may not survive. In a "slow" strategy, fewer offspring are produced, and parents invest more time and energy in their offspring. This strategy is typical when the environment is supportive, such that offspring usually survive. Strategies are matched to the environment where parents and offspring live.

3. *Research has identified three kinds of smiles, each addressing a unique social challenge and relying on different muscles in the face. Reward smiles are used to express happiness and involve lifting the eyebrows. Affiliative smiles are used to signal others about positive intentions and involve covering the teeth with the lips. Dominance smiles are used to assert social status and involve wrinkling the nose.

appeared for 100 ms and was followed by a masking stimulus for 300 ms. Participants reported the orientation of the target in the stimulus array.

In this case, words that indicate sequence (*then, next, finally, first, second, third*) are useful to help the reader remember that successive sentences are linked only by order, not specific content. Passage 16b, the original version of passage 8, shows how the addition of these words alerts the reader to the organization of the paragraph.

(16b) Experimental trials involved four events. *First*, a fixation circle appeared at the center of the screen for 500 ms. *Then* the stimulus array appeared for 100 ms and was followed by a masking stimulus for 300 ms. *Finally*, participants reported the orientation of the target in the stimulus array.

First, *then*, and *finally* provide the reader with explicit cues about the sequence of events and allow sequence to provide a sense of flow instead of content.

A Common Perspective

Smooth transitions between sentences help to create a paragraph that flows, but they aren't enough, as passage 17 shows:

(17) Speech perception involves not only audition but vision. Vision's impact on speech perception is evident in the McGurk effect, in which an audio track presenting *bah* is dubbed onto a video of a speaker saying *gah*, which a listener "hears" as *dah*. This perceptual error is less common in children with specific language impairment and in children with autism spectrum disorder. These disorders have been considered distinct but often involve overlapping deficits in language. This impaired language often leads to problems in academic success and in relationships with peers.

Each transition in this paragraph is reasonably smooth because the second sentence in each pair always leads with familiar information. But the paragraph as a whole is bizarre; it has a stream-of-consciousness feel associated with lyrics written by psychedelic musicians.

Passage 18a shows the same problem in less extreme form:

(18a) When people are trained to focus their attention by meditating, their performance improves on many tasks. For example, meditation training is associated with improved reading comprehension and more efficient attention. In addition, older adults trained in meditation recall more on memory span tasks. In both cases, meditation training helps reduce the influence of distracting stimuli that often undermine performance.

In terms of structure, passage 18a begins with a topic sentence describing benefits of meditation training, followed by sentences providing two examples of the benefits. The final sentence explains the process underlying improvements associated with meditation training. Although the structure is clear, passage 18a doesn't flow particularly well. Why? Passage 18b provides some clues. It has the same first and third sentences as passage 18a, but the second and fourth sentences (in italics) differ.

(18b) When people are trained to focus their attention by meditating, their performance improves on many tasks. *For example, following meditation training, college students comprehend more of what they read and attend to stimuli more efficiently.* In addition, older adults trained in meditation recall more on memory span tasks. *In both cases, individuals trained in meditation are better able to ignore distracting stimuli that often undermine performance.*

The difference is that each sentence in passage 18b adopts a common perspective or common viewpoint—each talks about training in terms of people who learn to meditate. In contrast, passage 18a alternates between talking about people trained to meditate (sentences 1 and 3) and meditation training as an abstract concept (sentences 2 and 4). Alternating between these two perspectives (people vs. abstraction) disrupts the sense of flow.

Passages 19a and 19b show the same pattern.

(19a) Following the death of a child, some parents shield their own grief from their spouse. Concealment of emotions is typically associated with greater experience of grief, not less. Apparently the effort parents invest in hiding their grief limits their ability to cope with that grief.

This brief paragraph doesn't flow well because it waffles between describing grief in terms of people's experiences (sentences 1 and 3) and as an abstraction (sentence 2). Passage 19b is better because it adopts a common viewpoint: Sentence 2 has been changed so that it, like the others, describes grief in terms of people's experiences.

(19b) Following the death of a child, some parents shield their own grief from their spouse. When parents hide their emotions in this way, they typically experience greater grief than if they had expressed their sense of loss. Apparently the effort parents invest in hiding their grief limits their ability to cope with that grief.

This passage flows because it consistently talks about parents' actions in dealing with grief. In other words, readers experience flow when the sentences in a paragraph share a common perspective in talking about the ideas from the topic sentence. To determine whether the sentences in a paragraph have a common viewpoint, compare their subjects. When sentences share a common viewpoint, the sentences typically have similar subjects. For example, in passage 18b, the subjects are *people, college students, older adults*, and *individuals*.

EXERCISE 4.6

Edit the sentences so they have a common perspective.

1. Sleep allows fragile memories to consolidate. This benefit is evident in memory for a range of materials, including emotions, textures, and speech. The converse is also true: When people are deprived of sleep, they often remember less accurately.
2. When intervention programs foster children's social-cognitive skills, children are less prone to antisocial behavior as adolescents. Such intervention programs work because they reduce hostile-attribution bias. And they have long-term effects: Antisocial behavior is reduced years after the intervention is over.
3. *Taking photographs of objects in a museum influences memory for those objects. On the one hand, recognition memory for the objects is greater when they are photographed than when they are not. On the other hand, people remember the audio description of those objects less accurately after they have photographed them.

LENGTH

One part of developing your voice is creating paragraphs reasonably consistent in length. For the three types of paragraphs described on pages 50–53, four to seven sentences are usually adequate. For example, when elaborating a topic sentence by providing supporting evidence, a six-sentence paragraph might

EXERCISE 4.7

Fix these paragraphs that are too long.

1. Cultures differ in their cognitive style, with Western individuals and East Asian individuals typically relying on analytic and holistic styles, respectively. On attention tasks, Westerners tend to focus on salient objects, but East Asians focus on relationships of objects. When categorizing objects or events, Westerners emphasize a single dimension, but East Asians emphasize overall similarity. In explaining people's behavior, Westerners stress traits of individuals, but East Asians stress the role of the situation. In reasoning, Westerners tend to be more analytical, but East Asians are more dialectical. Having observed others perform tasks, Westerners are more likely to perform the task "their own way," but East Asians often imitate what they've seen while observing others. In judging cause-effect relations, Westerners place greater emphasis on immediate causes, but East Asians place greater emphasis on more distal causes. Finally, in predicting the future, Westerners see the world as stable and expect current trends to continue, but East Asians see the world as changing and anticipate that current trends may be reversed.

2. According to the social information processing model, people's responses to social stimuli represent the product of several steps of processing. First, people attend selectively to certain features of the social stimulus but ignore other features. Second, they interpret the social stimulus—they try to understand what it means. Third, people evaluate their goals for the situation. Fourth, they retrieve from memory a behavioral response that fits the situation and their goals. Fifth, people decide if that response is appropriate. Sixth, if the response is appropriate, they enact it; otherwise, they search for another response. Seventh, they monitor how others respond to their behavior and, if necessary, update their database of behavioral responses.

3. *Parents commonly use three practices to prevent their young children from being injured at home. First, they teach their children rules about safety, such as "don't climb on the furniture." Second, they change their home environment to make it less hazardous; for example, they put medicines out of a child's reach and sight. Third, they supervise their children, watching them to be sure they do not put themselves at risk. Parents' beliefs about the risk of injury influence the practices they use. On the one hand, when parents believe their children are at little risk for injury, they're more likely to teach rules. On the other hand, when parents believe their children are at greater risk, they're more likely to change the home environment and supervise.

include four sentences that provide supporting information, plus topic and concluding sentences. The four sentences are usually enough to document the claims made in the topic sentence. More than four pieces of supporting information is often overkill: It makes the paragraph longer but doesn't make the argument more compelling (often because the additional evidence is weaker).

This length also works well for paragraphs contrasting alternative views or describing processes that unfold over time. For example, a six-sentence paragraph might include two sentences to describe each alternative, plus topic and concluding sentences. A seven-sentence paragraph could include three sentences for each alternative and a topic sentence, but no concluding sentence. In paragraphs describing processes, a six-sentence paragraph would include a topic sentence, plus descriptions of five steps. If there are more than five steps, it's probably best to create two groups of steps and devote a separate paragraph to each.

Of course, some paragraphs will naturally be longer than others due to the complexity of the controlling idea. That said, avoid paragraphs substantially longer or shorter than your average paragraph. In the midst of a slew of five- to seven-sentence paragraphs, three- and 15-sentence paragraphs cause trouble. Readers usually find much-longer-than-average paragraphs to be dense, in part because the length causes them to lose track of the paragraph's structure. They find much-shorter-than-average paragraphs to be underdeveloped and wonder why you didn't have more to say on the topic.

WRAP-UP

1. Make a paragraph's organization obvious by starting with a clear topic sentence and using the remaining sentences to flesh out the ideas in that topic sentence.

2. Make your writing flow by creating seamless transitions from one sentence to the next (always leading with familiar information) and by adopting a common perspective for all sentences in the paragraph.

3. Keep paragraphs relatively short (e.g., four to seven sentences) and avoid paragraphs substantially shorter or longer than your average paragraph.

FOR PRACTICE

1. Read just the topic sentences in an Introduction. Do they convey the gist of the author's argument? If not, revise them so they do.

2. Find paragraphs that don't flow well, either because transitions across sentences are awkward or because the sentences don't have a common perspective. Revise for better flow.

3. Search for paragraphs in an Introduction or Discussion section that seem unusually short or long compared to the others. Do they seem out of place? Why?

ANSWERS TO EXERCISES

Exercise 4.1

1. Topic = portion size; controlling idea = it influences how much food people eat.

2. Topic = landmarks; controlling idea = they help individuals orient to an environment and serve as markers for object locations.

3. Topic = children who experience lower-quality maternal care; controlling idea = they respond less adaptively to stress.

Exercise 4.2

1. Trait and state anxiety affect attention through different mechanisms. Trait anxiety is a by-product of an individual's personality and thus should affect attention through top-down processing. In contrast, state anxiety is linked to characteristics of specific situations and consequently should affect attention through bottom-up processing. (structure = comparison)

2. According to this model, experiencing darkness leads people to believe they are relatively invisible. In other words, darkness makes people feel anonymous. Consequently, in darkness people are more often dishonest and selfish. (structure = processes over time)

3. In health research, one of three measures is used to evaluate the life-saving impact of treatments. The simplest is the number of lives saved. Another is the number of life years gained. A third is the number of high-quality life years gained. (structure = supporting details)

Exercise 4.3

1. Trait and state anxiety affect attention through different mechanisms. Trait anxiety is a by-product of an individual's personality and thus should affect attention through top-down processing. In contrast, state anxiety is linked to

characteristics of specific situations and consequently should affect attention through bottom-up processing. *In other words, trait anxiety affects attention through top-down processes, but state anxiety affects attention through bottom-up processes.*

2. According to this model, experiencing darkness leads people to believe they are relatively invisible. In other words, darkness makes people feel anonymous. Consequently, in darkness people are more often dishonest and selfish. *Thus, darkness leads to anonymity, a process that then leads to unethical behavior.*

3. In health research, one of three measures is used to evaluate the life-saving impact of treatments. The simplest is the number of lives saved. Another is the number of life years gained. A third is the number of high-quality life years gained. *In summary, outcome measures include the number of lives saved along with life years gained and the number of quality years lived.*

Exercise 4.4

1. When people read, they fixate briefly on a word and then move on to the next word. These fixations tend to be longer in less skilled readers than in skilled readers.

2. People who believe they are vulnerable to disease rely on heuristics to minimize their risks. Typical heuristics include seeing themselves as more introverted (i.e., needing less social stimulation) and moving away from stimuli suggesting the presence of disease.

3. If there are domain-general resources, then performance on verbal tasks should be impaired when people perform a visual-spatial task simultaneously. This outcome has been reported in studies of Austrian, Belgian, and German undergraduates.

Exercise 4.5

1. The experiment included several phases linked by a cover story that the experiment concerned taste preferences. *First*, the participant was seated with two confederates and asked to complete questionnaires concerning mood and taste preferences. *Next*, while waiting for the experimenter to return, one confederate took a toy from a shelf and began throwing it to others; the participant received 5% of the throws in the ostracized condition but 33% in the included condition. *Finally*, the participant was asked to choose a type of hot sauce for a stranger; choices were labeled *mild*, *medium*, and *hot*.

2. According to life history theory, individuals differ in how they allocate resources to offspring. In a "fast" strategy, more offspring are produced, but parents invest relatively less time and energy in their offspring. This strategy is more common when the environment is harsh, such that offspring may not survive. *In contrast*, in a "slow" strategy, fewer offspring are produced, and parents invest more time and energy in their offspring. This strategy is typical when the environment is supportive, such that offspring usually survive. *Thus*, strategies are matched to the environment where parents and offspring live.

Exercise 4.6

I've revised each paragraph two ways, once relying on constructs and once relying on people.

1. Sleep allows fragile memories to consolidate. This benefit is evident in memory for a range of materials, including emotions, textures, and speech. The converse is also true: Sleep deprivation is associated with less accurate retention. OR

   During sleep, people's fragile memories consolidate. They have better memory for emotions, textures, and speech. The converse is also true: When people are deprived of sleep, they often remember less accurately.

2. Interventions designed to improve social-cognitive skills can reduce antisocial behavior during adolescence. Such intervention programs work because they reduce hostile-attribution bias. And they have long-term effects: Antisocial behavior is reduced years after the intervention is over. OR

   When intervention programs foster children's social-cognitive skills, children are less prone to antisocial behavior as adolescents. These programs work because participating children are less prone to interpret other people's actions as reflecting hostile intent. And they have long-term effects: Children are less prone to antisocial behavior years after the intervention is over.

Exercise 4.7

1. This eight-sentence paragraph provides seven examples of ways in which Westerners and East Asians differ in their thinking. That's overkill. I dropped the sentence about reasoning because it referred to Western reasoning as being analytical, which restates the controlling idea rather than illustrating it. I also deleted the sentence about the impact of watching others' performance because the difference was not readily captured in a single sentence. That left five examples and allowed me to add a concluding sentence, creating a seven-sentence paragraph:

Cultures differ in their cognitive style, with Western individuals and East Asian individuals typically relying on analytic and holistic styles, respectively. On attention tasks, Westerners tend to focus on salient objects, but East Asians focus on relationships of objects. When categorizing objects or events, Westerners emphasize a single dimension, but East Asians emphasize overall similarity. In explaining people's behavior, Westerners stress traits of individuals, but East Asians stress the role of the situation. In judging cause-effect relations, Westerners place greater emphasis on immediate causes, but East Asians place greater emphasis on more distal causes. Finally, in predicting future outcomes, Westerners see the world as stable and expect current trends to continue, but East Asians see the world as changing and anticipate that current trends may be reversed. Thus, across a range of perceptual, cognitive, and reasoning tasks, Western thinking is relatively analytic, but East Asian thinking is relatively holistic.

2. This eight-sentence paragraph has a topic sentence followed by sentences describing each of the seven steps of the model. Unlike the prior paragraph, each sentence is essential because it describes one step; deleting a step would misrepresent the model. Consequently, I broke this into two five-sentence paragraphs, one devoted to the initial steps that deal with interpreting the stimulus and a second devoted to the later steps that deal with responses:

According to the social information processing model, people's responses to social stimuli represent the product of several steps of processing. The initial steps involve encoding a stimulus. First, people attend selectively to certain features of the social stimulus but ignore other features. Second, they interpret the social stimulus—they try to understand what it means. Third, people evaluate their goals for the situation.

Having interpreted a situation, processing now shifts to determining an appropriate response. First, people retrieve from memory a behavioral response that fits the situation and their goals. Second, they decide if that response is appropriate. Third, if the response is appropriate, they enact it; otherwise, they search for another response. Fourth, they monitor how others respond to their behavior and, if necessary, update their database of behavioral responses.

5

Framing an Introduction

A well-written research report builds on the skills that were the focus of Lessons 1 through 4: writing compelling sentences and coherent paragraphs. These skills are particularly important in crafting an Introduction. If the Introduction fails to provide a convincing rationale for the study, the editor will probably reject the manuscript. In fact, many editors and reviewers form a preliminary evaluation of the manuscript based on the Introduction alone, asking questions like these: Is the issue timely and critical to the field? Is the author's approach fresh and likely to offer bold new insights? Are the methods well suited to answer the questions that motivated the work? When reviewers read an Introduction and find themselves answering "no" more often than "yes," they're not likely to be enthusiastic about the paper. So, it's worth investing more time, effort, and planning in this section of the manuscript than any other.

The Introduction has three parts. The first introduces the topic of your work and establishes why it's important. The second provides the rationale for your work. And the third states the hypotheses and how they are evaluated in your work.

STATING THE PROBLEM (AND HOOKING THE READER!)

The first part of the Introduction—typically one paragraph and occasionally two—is designed to introduce the topic of the study and pique the reader's curiosity. This first paragraph is your chance to convince the reader that your manuscript is different from the thousands of papers published in psychology journals every year (and the thousands more that are submitted but not published).

Too often research reports begin by describing the state of the research literature; sentence 1a illustrates this approach:

(1a)   Social psychologists have studied many types of cooperation but have ignored interactions that require physical cooperation.

This approach makes your manuscript seem run-of-the-mill. A better strategy is to begin by talking about people (or other animals) and their behavior. One way is to mention behaviors that are familiar yet poorly understood.

(1b)   When people enter a building, others often hold the door for them. Although such interactions are commonplace, we know little about forms of social interaction like these that involve physical cooperation.

Sentence 1b introduces the topic with an example familiar to all readers; the fact that we know little about such a familiar phenomenon is a good way to "hook" the reader.

Another effective strategy is to begin with a rhetorical question for the reader to ponder. Sentence 2a shows an unimaginative state-of-the-literature introductory sentence:

(2a)   In a review of the literature on choice overload, Harris, Becker, and Hall (2010) concluded that people enjoy having many alternatives from which to choose, yet they often find such choices less satisfying.

Sentence 2b is a variant that begins with a rhetorical question:

(2b)   Suppose you want to buy a new camera. Would you prefer to shop at a store that has three cameras in your price range or a store that has 12? Research on choice overload suggests you will prefer the store with more choices but be less satisfied with a camera purchased there (Harris, Becker, & Hall, 2010).

A third useful strategy is to start with an interesting statistic. Sentence 3a introduces the topic in a straightforward but uninspired manner:

(3a)   Research on the cognitive processes underlying reading has focused on reading English, which is problematic because English is an unusual language in that spellings and sounds are not linked consistently (Moreau, Horvat, Mertens, & Gruber, 2008).

In contrast, sentence 3b starts with a statistic that establishes a striking imbalance between the number of people who read English and the number of studies conducted on reading English:

(3b)   Less than 10% of the world's population reads English, yet 90% of the published articles on reading have involved English-speaking readers (Olsen & Nagy, 2012); this is potentially problematic because English is an unusual language in that spellings and sounds are not linked consistently (Moreau, Horvat, Mertens, & Gruber, 2008).

A fourth strategy is to begin with a case study or anecdote—a brief description of a person (or persons) or an event that illustrates the phenomenon of interest. Sentence 4a is a typical uninspired opening sentence.

(4a)   Some problems are solved through an "aha experience" in which the solution comes suddenly and effortlessly (Posselt & Krupa, 2018).

In contrast, passage 4b starts with an anecdote that brings life to the aha experience:

(4b)   In 1949, 16 firefighters were on the verge of being trapped by a forest fire. One of them, Wagner Dodge, unexpectedly realized that by setting a small, controllable fire, he could clear a path for him and his coworkers to escape. Dodge's solution illustrates an "aha experience"—an answer to a problem that occurs suddenly and effortlessly (Posselt & Krupa, 2018).

These approaches often engage a reader because they deal with people behaving, thinking, or feeling, which is the focus of psychological science. In other words, the research literature is a means to an end: understanding why people behave, think, and feel as they do. Emphasizing that end is a better way to start a paper than emphasizing the means.

EXERCISE 5.1

Improve these introductory sentences by adding an example, a rhetorical question, an eye-popping statistic, or a gripping anecdote.

1. Research on memory shows that emotion-laden events are remembered more accurately than neutral events, but the relative accuracy of recall of positive versus negative events is not well established.
2. Studies of the impact of a group's heterogeneity on performance suggest benefits (e.g., different perspectives yield greater creativity) as well as drawbacks (e.g., greater effort involved in coordinating diverse workers).
3. Many studies have been conducted to determine whether workplace wellness programs are more effective when they reward employees for healthy behavior or penalize them for unhealthy behavior.
4. *Advertising research reveals that the effectiveness of product endorsements by celebrities depends on the familiarity, trustworthiness, and credibility of the celebrity.

PROVIDING THE RATIONALE FOR YOUR WORK

This section of the Introduction is sometimes known as the "review of the literature," but I believe that phrase is misleading—it implies that you should provide a general overview of a body of research. In fact, this section has a precise aim: to develop the rationale for your work, typically through a series of steps in which you identify what's known as well as what remains unknown or what is controversial. Of course, in describing the rationale, you will refer to research that's been done, but the aim is specific: to document—with research findings—the claims you make in the rationale for your study.

This section of the manuscript can take many forms, reflecting differences in the kind of research being reported. Common types of research are reporting a brand-new phenomenon or effect, providing evidence that promotes greater understanding of a phenomenon, or testing alternative accounts of a phenomenon (Kendall, Silk, & Chu, 2000). Each of these kinds of research is motivated with a unique set of arguments, but the rationale usually begins broadly, establishing what's known and unknown, and then zeros in on the focus of the research.

Regardless of the kind of research you're reporting, a good way to begin writing this section of the Introduction is to list each step of your argument, briefly. For example, passage 5a includes four steps that provide the rationale for a study in which aggressive adolescents learned how to interpret emotions conveyed by facial expressions.

(5a)

   a.   Facial expressions are cues to people's behavior.

   b.   Aggressive teens misinterpret these cues (hostile bias).

   c.   These teens can be trained to interpret facial expressions more accurately.

   d.   Evidence is weak—little external validity.

Next, using the guidelines described in Lesson 4, translate each of these ideas into a topic sentence:

(5b)

   a.   People often use others' facial expressions to understand their behavior.

   b.   Most people are reasonably accurate in the inferences they draw from others' facial expressions, but aggressive adolescents are not: They tend to infer hostile intentions from neutral or ambiguous facial expressions.

   c.   Intervention studies have been successful in teaching aggressive adolescents how to interpret others' facial expressions more accurately.

   d.   Despite the success of intervention studies, there is no evidence that the improved recognition of facial expressions generalizes to adolescents' interactions with families and peers.

The next step is to flesh out the claim made in each of these topic sentences, in a paragraph or two. For example, sentence c in passage 5b would be followed by sentences describing the kinds of intervention studies that have been conducted; sentence d in passage 5b would be followed by sentences showing that intervention studies have focused exclusively on adolescents' recognition of facial expressions in laboratory settings.

As you develop these paragraphs, it's essential that you follow some basic guidelines.

EXERCISE 5.2

Find an article on the web and "reverse engineer" the basic argument developed in the Introduction. In other words, list the steps in the author's argument that were used (or should have been used) to generate the topic sentences.

Put Issues, Ideas, and Findings in the Foreground and Studies and Scientists in the Background

Your rationale will be most effective if you frame it in terms of the issues at stake and not the studies in the literature (or the scientists who conducted the studies). Said differently, in reviewing the literature, you need to establish what's known and what isn't; that description should be fact oriented, not study oriented. Passage 6a, for example, illustrates a study-oriented description of a literature.

> (6a)   There is an extensive literature on gender differences in mathematical performance. Schneider (2000) presented a range of addition and subtraction problems to first- and second-grade students; girls responded more accurately and faster than boys. Murphy (2011) reported that for seventh graders taking the mathematical part of the Scholastic Aptitude Test, which measures mathematical reasoning, boys had a mean score of 416 compared to a mean of 386 for girls. Sordi (1987) found that, for sixth-grade students, boys had greater scores than girls on the mathematical problem-solving scale of the Canadian Test of Basic Skills. Bast (2013) tested third to sixth graders on a range of arithmetic tasks, including subtraction, multiplication, and numerosity comparison; in all cases, girls outperformed boys.

The passage cites four studies, with each described in terms of the children's grade level, the tasks, and the findings. It's difficult reading and puts the burden of interpreting these findings on the reader. In contrast, passage 6b is an outcome-oriented version of the passage where the text summarizes the state of the literature, citing relevant studies.

> (6b)   There is an extensive literature on gender differences in mathematical performance. Boys typically achieve greater scores on measures of mathematical problem solving (Murphy, 2011; Sordi, 1987), but girls have greater scores on tests of arithmetical computation (Bast, 2013; Schneider, 2000).

And by applying some of the tips from previous lessons, we might summarize everything in a single sentence:

> (6c)   A paradox in the study of mathematical cognition is that boys typically achieve greater scores on measures of mathematical

problem solving, but girls have greater scores on tests of arithmetical computation (Murphy, 2011; Schneider, 2000).

Of course, it's common for the rationale you develop in an Introduction to hinge on a critical study or two. You'll need to describe these in greater detail, often by name. But this sort of description should be the exception; when using the literature to document the claims in your rationale, put the studies in the background and emphasize the relevant findings.

Be Fair in Describing the Literature

When you describe previous research that provides the background to your work, be sure to provide a complete and unbiased account. Incomplete or

EXERCISE 5.3

Revise these paragraphs to put the findings in the foreground.

1. Skill at learning a second language (L2) depends on several factors. Wilson (2009) showed that adults with greater phonetic ability were better at learning a second language. Joyner (2007) reported a significant correlation between L2 skill and grammatical sensitivity. DeWolff (1987) found that scores on a phonological memory task predicted performance on a simulated language-learning task.

2. The effects of cognitive load on performance are inconsistent. López (1988) reported that participants made more errors on an arithmetic task when they were simultaneously generating letters randomly. Kim, King, Novak, and Campbell (2000) found that adolescents were slower to judge whether a stimulus was a letter when they were also monitoring a series of words for the presence of a target word. However, Hester, Fischer, and Lee (1990) showed that golfers putted more accurately when they were also judging whether background tones were high or low pitched. Moore and Turner (2011) demonstrated more rapid learning of perceptual categories when participants were also remembering a sequence of digits.

3. *Research has revealed several factors that influence whether youth engage in cyberbullying. Galić and Švajda (2012) reported that, for middle school students, cyberbullies tended to be students who bullied offline (i.e., face-to-face) as well. Rankin and Wolbrink (2014) found that cyberbullying was more common among high school students who believed that bullying and aggression are acceptable behaviors. In a study by Yu, Wolters, and Tarr (2017), cyberbullying was less frequent when middle school and high school students believed that their teachers were fair and supportive. Finally, Templin (2016) observed that cyberbullying was less common among high school students whose parents monitored their behavior.

biased descriptions of relevant research always annoy readers. In other words, readers will definitely notice if your review omits work that isn't favorable to the arguments you develop.

In describing work it's essential that you're fair. For example, it's fine to identify shortcomings in prior work, but be objective in your criticisms. And never engage in ad hominem arguments (where you attack the person doing the work, not the work itself). An effective rationale for research touches on all of the necessary points, briefly, and in a manner that leaves people on all sides of an issue reasonably satisfied that the work has been presented accurately.

Cite Previous Work Selectively

As you draw on the literature to frame your arguments, you may be tempted to cite all (or most) relevant studies. Don't! Exhaustively citing the literature has three problems. First, the aim of this part of your paper is not to describe the literature per se (as you would in a review paper) but to establish the logical and empirical basis for the arguments that motivate your study. For this purpose, you simply need to show that each of your arguments is backed by evidence; you needn't cite all of the supporting evidence. Said differently, the argument isn't necessarily more convincing if you cite five studies instead of just one or two. Second, many journals limit the number of references, a practice that forces you to be selective. Third, the standard practice of citing work by author and date of publication adds information to a sentence that interferes with the reader's comprehension of your text. For example, sentence 7a is easier to read (and much shorter) than sentence 7b.

(7a)   Early and late in life, people are prone to perseverative errors: Infants search for an object where it was hidden previously despite seeing it hidden elsewhere, and elderly adults sort cards using an old rule that has since been replaced.

(7b)   Early and late in life, people are prone to perseverative errors (Hernández, Walker, & Hansen, 1975; Kowalski, Allen, Hill, & Flores, 2002, 2009): Infants search for an object where it was hidden previously despite seeing it hidden elsewhere (Hughes, Long, & Foster, 1999; Parker & Stewart, 2010; Taylor, Campbell, & Tanaka, 1999), and elderly adults sort cards using an old rule that has since been replaced (Meyer, Schmidt, & Durand, 2005; Rivera & Cook, 2008).

A general rule is that two citations should be adequate to bolster each step in your argument; three or more is overkill. When selecting studies to cite, one good choice is a recent review article that summarizes the relevant evidence. If a recent review is not available, you could cite an older review along with a recent study showing the same effect. Feel free to cite your own work, but only if it provides direct evidence and if it's the best evidence. Reviewers typically are critical of gratuitous self-citations.

Because citations are not part of the argument per se, I recommend putting them at the end of a sentence instead of scattering them throughout the sentence, as was done in sentence 8a.

(8a)   Some of the factors that influence how people vote include their values (Peeters, Jackson, & Carter, 1992), demographic features (Dubois & Anderson, 2004), and the presence of negative affect like fear or anger (Moore & Hernández, 2013).

The first two citations in sentence 8a are hurdles: Readers must jump them and find where your text resumes. In contrast, by placing the citations at the end, as in sentence 8b, the reader's path to understanding your sentence is uninterrupted by citations.

(8b)   Some of the factors that influence how people vote include their values, demographic features, and the presence of negative affect like fear or anger (Dubois & Anderson, 2004; Moore & Hernández, 2013; Peeters, Jackson, & Carter, 1992).

This practice does move the supporting evidence a few words from the relevant text, but readers who are really invested in the topic can make the links. The remaining readers don't really care and are grateful that you've made the text easier to read. Of course, if the aim of the sentence is to contrast two views or hypotheses, you should separate those citations because they support different claims.

Many young writers are nervous about citing research selectively; they fear doing so will antagonize individuals who review their manuscripts. In other words, young scientists worry that if they neglect to cite Evans, Rossi, and Van Dyk (2013) and Evans, Rossi, or Van Dyk happens to review their manuscript, he or she will recommend the manuscript be rejected. In my experience, you needn't worry about this. As mentioned earlier, reviewers object strongly to a biased presentation of the literature, but they don't respond harshly to the absence of individual studies per se. They may suggest you cite additional studies. If the editor endorses that suggestion, go ahead and include the suggested studies. (And because your original manuscript has relatively few citations, adding two to three more won't be a problem.)

STATING (OR RESTATING) THE HYPOTHESES AND LINKING THEM TO THE DESIGN

The last paragraph (or two) of the Introduction has a special role—you state your hypotheses, predictions, or expectations and link them to your study's design. In most Introductions, you will have stated the hypotheses already; this paragraph simply reminds the reader of them. However, the critical function of the paragraph is to show that your methods will provide evidence you can use to evaluate the hypotheses.

Let's return to the study outlined on pages 73 designed to determine whether aggressive adolescents' improved recognition of facial expressions generalized to interactions with families and peers. The paragraphs leading up to the final paragraph have established that aggressive adolescents can learn to recognize facial expressions more accurately but that most studies have evaluated such learning in limited contexts (e.g., recognizing facial expressions in static photos). Thus, the objective of this final paragraph is to remind the reader of the aim of the work (to determine whether adolescents' learning will generalize to interactions) and to explain how this was tested. Passage 9 illustrates one possibility:

(9)   The aim of the present work was to determine whether adolescents' improved recognition of facial expressions following training would generalize to a more realistic setting. Aggressive adolescents were assigned randomly to either a control condition or an intervention condition. In the latter, adolescents were trained to distinguish photos depicting individuals who look happy from those who look angry. Following training, all participants judged whether facial expressions depicted happiness or anger in still photographs of novel adults and then in brief videos (with audio omitted) of unfamiliar adolescents interacting with an adult. If training is effective and generalizes beyond the immediate training environment, then adolescents who participated in the training condition should judge facial expressions in novel photos and in the videos more accurately than do adolescents in the control condition.

Notice that passage 9 begins by stating the aims of the experiment, includes three sentences that provide an overview of the method, and ends with a statement of the expected pattern of results.

Passage 10 is another example. In this case, the Introduction has established that executive function has three components for adolescents and adults but that its structure is less established in younger children.

(10)   The present study was conducted to determine whether the structure of executive function changes during childhood. Children at two ages—4 and 8 years—were tested on tasks measuring the inhibitory, shifting, and updating components of executive function that are found with adolescents and adults. We expected that the pattern of correlations across tasks would reveal the mature three-factor structure for 8-year-olds but a single, undifferentiated structure for 4-year-olds.

Passage 10 follows the same template as passage 9: It begins by describing the study's purpose, then provides a glimpse of the methods—just enough so the reader can understand how they were used to evaluate the hypotheses—and ends by describing the predicted pattern of results.

One common mistake in writing this paragraph is to use present or future tense. In fact, you're describing events that have already occurred, so the past tense is appropriate. Another common mistake is to provide too much detail about methods. You should provide the minimum amount of detail about design and procedure for readers to understand what you did and what kinds of results provide informative evidence. For example, passage 10 does not include information about the specific tasks used to measure executive function because it is not essential for understanding the logic of the study.

To end this lesson, I remind you that the Introduction is one of the two most important sections in the manuscript. (The Results section is the other.) If your Introduction is really well written, readers will be so excited at the end of this section that they'll jump directly to the Results to see if the study worked out as you expected.

EXERCISE 5.4

Create an Introduction-ending paragraph from the information provided.

1.   Are positive and negative events remembered equally well?

Hypothesis: Because negative outcomes lead to more processing of details, we expect negative events to be recalled more accurately.

Method: In the spring of the school year, we asked students at four high schools to recall the scores of their school's football games from the previous fall. Each student received a list of all games with the opponent's name provided; students listed the number of points scored by each team. To control for exposure to game-related information, students were asked to estimate, on 7-point scales, their

(Continued)

(Continued)

interest in their high school football team and their attendance at the previous fall's games.

2. Do people's responses to stressful daily events predict whether they develop depression?

Hypothesis: People who respond routinely to stressful daily events by becoming upset, hostile, or nervous are at greater risk for developing depressive symptoms.

Method: College students were tested twice during the academic year. In the second month of the fall semester, they came to the laboratory and completed a measure of depressive symptoms. In the week that followed this visit, every evening they completed online measures of (a) the different stressors they had experienced that day (e.g., "had an argument with a friend") and (b) the extent to which they had experienced positive and negative emotions during the day. During the last month of the academic year, they returned to the lab and completed the measure of depressive symptoms again.

3. *Does feeling insecure financially influence people's reports of physical pain?

Hypothesis: Feeling insecure about income and employment can lead people to report experiencing greater pain.

Method: Adults recruited online were assigned randomly to one of two conditions. In one condition, they were asked to write a paragraph describing a time in their life when their financial situation was insecure (e.g., they lost a job, they had trouble playing bills). In another condition, participants were asked to write a paragraph describing a time when their financial situation was secure (e.g., they had just taken a job with good pay, they had received a large bonus). Then participants completed questionnaires measuring (a) how much physical pain they were experiencing, (b) their mood, (c) their personality, and (d) demographic variables.

WRAP-UP

1. Use a good example, rhetorical question, surprising fact, or anecdote to hook the reader into reading your paper.

2. As you structure the argument that motives your work, put the evidence in the foreground (and the studies yielding the evidence in the background), present the evidence accurately, and cite evidence selectively.

3. In the last paragraph (or two) of the Introduction, describe the hypotheses and how they're evaluated in the study.

FOR PRACTICE

1. Read the first paragraph or two of several articles. Do they begin with effective hooks? If so, what makes the hook effective? If not, rewrite them so they are more likely to grab the reader.

2. Find paragraphs that are study oriented; rewrite them to be evidence oriented.

3. Read the final paragraph(s) of the Introduction from several articles; decide whether they provide a clear description of hypotheses and how those hypotheses are to be evaluated in the study.

ANSWERS TO EXERCISES

Exercise 5.1

1. Following the championship match of the World Cup, fans of the winning team leave with many positive memories whereas fans of the losing team have many negative memories. Research indicates that both groups of fans will recall the match more accurately than a neutral observer, but evidence is inconsistent concerning whether fans of the winning or losing team will recall the match more accurately.

2. You've just finished your PhD and are choosing between two positions, each involving an excellent group of 10 scientists. One group includes experts from a few closely related disciplines, and the other includes scientists from a broad range of disciplines. You want to join the most productive group; which should you choose? In fact, studies of the impact of a group's heterogeneity on performance suggest benefits (e.g., different perspectives yield greater creativity) as well as drawbacks (e.g., greater effort involved in coordinating diverse workers).

3. Unhealthy employees are expensive for U.S. companies. For example, a typical smoker costs his or her company more than $3,000 annually in increased health care costs, greater absenteeism, and reduced productivity. Consequently, there has been much interest in determining whether workplace wellness programs are more effective when they reward employees for healthy behavior or penalize them for unhealthy behavior.

Exercise 5.3

1. Skill at learning a second language (L2) depends on several factors, including phonetic ability (Wilson, 2009), grammatical sensitivity (Joyner, 2007), and phonological memory (DeWolff, 1987).

2. The effects of cognitive load on performance are inconsistent. On the one hand, simultaneously performing a second task (e.g., generating letters, remembering digits) often impairs performance: People err more often on arithmetic tasks and respond more slowly when judging whether a stimulus is a letter when they are simultaneously generating letters randomly (Kim, King, Novak, & Campbell, 2000; López, 1988). On the other hand, performing a second task occasionally improves performance: Golfers putt more accurately, and people learn perceptual categories more rapidly (Hester, Fischer, & Lee, 1990; Moore & Turner, 2011).

Exercise 5.4

1. To determine the impact of an event's emotional valence on memory for that event, we asked students to recall the scores of football games in which their school's team had played. Because negative outcomes lead to more processing of details, we anticipated students would remember scores of losses more accurately than scores of wins.

2. The aim of our study was to examine the link between a person's response to stressful situations and risk for developing depressive symptoms. At the beginning of the academic year, college students completed a measure of depressive symptoms. Then, for a week they reported their daily experiences of stressful life events, positive emotions, and negative emotions. Finally, at the end of the year, they again completed a measure of depressive symptoms. We expected that people who initially reported greater stress and greater negative affect would report greater depressive symptoms at the end of the school year (controlling for symptoms at the beginning of the year).

6

Reporting Results

The data are in, the analyses are complete, and the findings look promising. It's time to write! You'll probably have written a draft of an Introduction when you proposed the research. I recommend you reread this material but then begin writing your paper with the Results section. Why? This section—more than any other—will make or break the paper. In other words, if the results aren't compelling, no amount of fussing with the Introduction or Discussion sections is likely to rescue the paper.

As you write this section, stick to the storytelling approach I've emphasized throughout this book and that you used to write the Introduction. Tell the reader what happened and use the outcome of statistical tests to support your account. Keep the results in the foreground and the analyses in the background. In other words, statistical tests are to the Results section what citations are to the Introduction and Discussion sections—they aren't the story but document the story.

GETTING STARTED

You probably have a stack of analyses and may be tempted to start writing by summarizing them, one by one. Don't! That approach ends up highlighting the analyses themselves instead of the key findings. A better path to good storytelling of results is to think of this section as a photo essay. Books in this genre include evocative photographs surrounded by a modest amount of explanatory text. Applied to the Results section, this means you'll include a few graphs or tables that depict the important findings along with text that walks the reader through the findings and provides the necessary statistical documentation.

The first step is to pick the evocative photos. Of course, typically these won't be photos per se but graphs or tables. These should depict the essential findings—those you'd be eager to share with friends and colleagues so they can see why you're so excited.

Many writers believe the choice of a graph or table is simply personal preference (or whether an author has access to fancy graphing software), but that's not true. Graphs are generally better than tables, particularly when the pattern of results is important. Most readers can detect patterns much more quickly in a graph than a table. For example, Figure 1 and Table 4 show the same numbers, but the pattern—the dependent variable increases more rapidly in Condition A than in Condition B—leaps out of the figure but not the table.[1]

Tables are preferred in three circumstances. The first is to present many correlation coefficients: A matrix such as that shown in Table 5 allows many correlations to be presented economically.

FIGURE 1

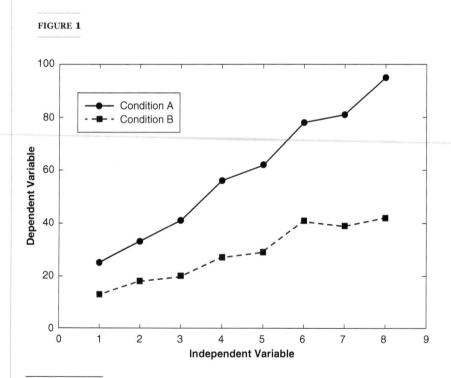

---

[1] For simplicity, neither Figure 1 nor Table 4 includes measures of variability. In practice, this information should always be included in graphs and tables.

TABLE 4   **Effect of the Independent Variable on the Dependent Variable, Separately for Conditions A and B**

	Independent Variable							
Condition	1	2	3	4	5	6	7	8
A	25	33	41	56	62	78	81	95
B	13	18	20	27	29	41	39	42

TABLE 5   **Descriptive Statistics and Bivariate Correlations**

Measure	M	SD	1	2	3
1. Self-control	0.79	0.14	—		
2. Verbal intelligence	104.10	12.60	.23*	—	
3. Socioeconomic status	32.15	11.50	.05	.28*	—
4. Antisocial behavior	0.90	0.18	−.37**	−.24*	−.07

$*p < .05, **p < .01.$

A second circumstance is when the reader needs to know exact values of variables instead of patterns. One common situation is a table showing the results of multiple regression analyses, where readers are interested in the specific values of beta weights; Table 6 is an example.

A third circumstance is to show results from an experiment that involves multiple dependent variables or from multiple experiments with the same variable. Table 7 demonstrates the efficient presentation of outcomes for several

TABLE 6   **Multiple Regression Analysis Predicting Math Achievement in High School**

Predictor	β	SE
Grade 5 verbal IQ	.10	.01**
Grade 5 nonverbal IQ	.18	.02**
Household income	.05	.03*
Parents' education	.15	.02**
Total R^2	.23	

$*p < .05, **p < .01 (N = 153).$

TABLE 7   **Findings From Experiment 1**

	Condition	
Variable	Control	Choice
Support income redistribution	3.7 (1.1)	2.4 (1.2)*
Personal agency causes outcomes	3.5 (0.9)	4.8 (1.4)*
Concerns about unequal wealth	5.2 (1.7)	3.3 (1.5)*

Note: Each scored on a 1–7 scale, where 7 = strongly agree; standard deviations in parentheses.
*Means differ significantly, $ts(38) \geq 8.21$, $\eta^2 \geq .09$, $p < .01$.

variables. In comparison, a graph showing this information would be complex, either involving multiple panels (one for each variable) or including multiple Y axes. Of course, in an experiment with multiple dependent variables where you're interested in the pattern for each one, you may need to bite the bullet and go with a complex figure.

Having decided which format will work best for your results, create a working version of a graph or table. Just a rough version will do for now; you can tweak it later.

EXERCISE 6.1

Decide whether these results are best suited for a graph or table and then construct that graph or table.

1. In an experiment designed to evaluate the impact of an intervention on adolescents' consumption of soda, half of the participants were assigned to the intervention condition and half to a control condition. Consumption of soda was measured before the intervention began and when it ended, as well as 3 and 6 months after it ended. For adolescents in the intervention condition, consumption (defined as the number of 20-ounce drinks/week) was 8.6, 3.2, 4.5, and 7.5 at the four measurements; for adolescents in the control condition, corresponding values were 8.9, 6.9, 7.6, and 8.0.

2. In an experiment on the impact of rejection on mood, participants tossed a ball with two other people who were actually confederates of the experimenter. Participants received the ball often in the included condition, but not in the rejection condition. All sessions were video recorded and scored later for facial expressions of negative emotions such as anger or sadness. After 5 minutes of ball tossing, participants in both conditions rated their sadness on a 7-point scale

in which larger numbers indicated greater sadness. Finally, participants were asked whether they would be willing to take part in another experiment with the confederates. The video records showed that 18% of participants who were included displayed negative emotion compared with 85% of participants who were rejected. Average ratings of sadness were 2.5 and 5.6 for included and rejected participants, respectively. When asked to participate in another experiment with the confederates, 78% of included participants agreed, but only 15% of rejected participants agreed.

3. *To determine the impact of repeated testing on retention, college students studied each of 45 pairs consisting of a Croatian noun and its English translation. On the first presentation of each pair, participants were allowed to study for 10 sec. On subsequent presentations, the Croatian word was presented and participants had 5 sec to respond with its English translation. If they did so correctly, the next pair was presented; otherwise, the English translation was presented with the Croatian word for 5 sec of additional study time. For one third of the pairs, the pair of words was presented until participants responded correctly once; for another third, the pair was presented until participants responded correctly twice; for the remaining third, the pair was presented until participants responded correctly four times. In a final recall test, all 50 Croatian words were presented individually and participants attempted to provide the English translation. Participants were randomly assigned to have final recall either 0, 24, 72, or 144 hours after learning the pairs. For pairs on which participants responded correctly once, the percentage of English translations recalled correctly was 60, 36, 16, and 12, at 0, 24, 72, and 144 hours, respectively, since learning the pairs. For pairs on which participants responded correctly twice, corresponding figures were 68, 46, 24, and 18; for pairs on which participants responded correctly four times, corresponding figures were 72, 53, 29, and 21.

DESCRIBING THE FINDINGS

With the graphs and tables selected, it's time for the text that will "walk the reader" through your results. As I said earlier, the best way to guide your readers is to tell a story, citing the analyses as necessary to support what you have to say. At this point, focus on the text for each graph or table individually. Don't worry about weaving everything together to form a coherent Results section; that comes later.

In the next few pages, I illustrate this storytelling approach with two common kinds of findings.

Findings From Experimental Research

In experimental research, hypotheses usually concern relations between means, such as expecting one mean to be greater than another or expecting means to increase as a function of changes in an independent variable.

Hypotheses like these are often tested with analyses of variance. For example, imagine an experiment in which participants read sentences presented on a computer screen. For half the sentences, the meaning was straightforward, and for half the meaning was ambiguous. In addition, some participants read sentences presented in a familiar font, and some read sentences in an unfamiliar font. We hypothesize that reading will be slower when sentences are ambiguous and appear in an unfamiliar font; we also hypothesize that these two factors will interact, such that reading is particularly slow when sentences are ambiguous *and* in an unfamiliar font.

A conventional way to determine whether the findings (shown in Figure 2) are consistent with these hypotheses would be to compute a two-way analysis of variance (ANOVA), with font as a between-subjects variable and type of sentence as a within-subjects variable. One common way to describe the outcome of such an ANOVA appears in passage 1a:

(1a)   We conducted a two-way analysis of variance on the reading times shown in Figure 2 with type of font (familiar, unfamiliar) as a between-subjects variable and type of sentence (unambiguous, ambiguous) as a within-subjects variable. The main effect of type of font was significant, $F(1, 22) = 56.33$, $\eta^2 = .18$, $p < .01$, as was the main effect of type of sentence, $F(1, 22) = 315.50$, $\eta^2 = .67$, $p < .01$.

FIGURE **2**

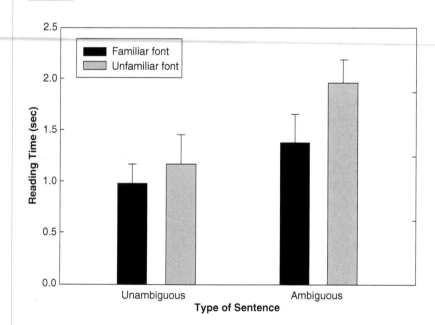

The interaction between type of sentence and type of font was significant, $F(1, 22) = 9.50$, $\eta^2 = .02$, $p < .01$. Simple-effects analyses showed that the effect of type of sentence was significant for both familiar fonts, $F(1, 22) = 108.0$, $p < .01$, and unfamiliar fonts, $F(1, 22) = 216.75$, $p < .01$.

Passage 1a is a good example of *statisticalese*—it focuses on describing the outcomes of the ANOVA but doesn't tell the reader what happened in the experiment. Compare with passage 1b:

(1b)   Reading times are shown in Figure 2. As hypothesized, reading times were greater for unfamiliar fonts, $F(1, 22) = 56.33$, $\eta^2 = .18$, and for ambiguous sentences, $F(1, 22) = 315.50$, $\eta^2 = .67$. Furthermore, the predicted interaction was significant, $F(1, 22) = 9.50$, $\eta^2 = .02$: Ambiguous sentences took more time to read with familiar and unfamiliar fonts, $Fs(1, 22) \geq 108.0$, but the effect was greater for unfamiliar fonts.

Passage 1b tells the reader what happened in the experiment. Statistical documentation appears, but it doesn't drive the sentences; instead, it's in the background where it doesn't interfere with the story line. For example, passage 1a refers to a main effect of font type, but passage 1b tells the reader that participants took longer to read unfamiliar fonts. Similarly, *interaction* appears in both passages, as a component of the ANOVA in passage 1a but as a distinct pattern of means in passage 1b. In short, don't list significant effects; instead describe what happened and document each outcome statistically.

Several other small features make passage 1b easier to read. First, the outcomes are linked to the hypotheses. Second, the structure of the ANOVA isn't described. If your description of the design in the Method section is clear, readers who really care can infer the ANOVA's structure. Third, p values are missing; as I describe on page 99, they've been reported elsewhere. Fourth, the results of the tests of simple main effects were summarized—$Fs \geq 108$—instead of listing the F values separately.

Another trick for better storytelling of results is to describe findings in terms of what participants did, not in terms of the conditions of the experiment. Sentence 2a illustrates the familiar ANOVA-oriented description you should avoid:

(2a)   There was a significant main effect for type of video game, $F(1, 65) = 6.24$, $\eta^2 = .08$.

Sentence 2b is better because it emphasizes the finding, not the statistical test.

(2b)   Cheating was greater in the violent video game condition than in the nonviolent video game condition, $F(1, 65) = 6.24$, $\eta^2 = .08$.

But we can do better if we phrase the <u>outcome in terms of what partici-pants did in the conditions</u>:

(2c)   Participants cheated more when they played a violent video game than when they played a nonviolent video game, $F(1, 65) = 6.24$, $\eta^2 = .08$.

Sentence 2c is easy to read because, unlike sentence 2b, the reader doesn't need to remember what happened in the conditions; the text reminds the reader. In addition, sentence 2c has the properties of clear writing described in Lesson 1: The sentence is organized around actors and their actions (partici-pants cheating).

Sentences 3a and 3b also illustrate the difference between a descrip-tion based on conditions and one based on what participants did in those conditions:

(3a)   Errors were greater in the high-load condition than in the low- and no-load conditions, $F(2, 48) = 4.17$, $\eta^2 = .05$.

(3b)   Participants erred more often when they performed the task under high load than under low or no load, $F(2, 48) = 4.17$, $\eta^2 = .05$.

EXERCISE 6.2

Rewrite the paragraph about the results so it describes the outcomes of the experi-ments, not the ANOVAs.

1.   Background: College students attempted to solve reasoning problems presented on a computer screen. Periodically a probe appeared on the screen asking them how focused they were on the task (1 = not at all; 5 = completely focused). They solved two sets of problems, separated by an hour. During this time, students in the training condition were given tips for focusing their attention; students in the control condition were given tips for not gaining weight. The hypothesis was that students in the training condition will improve their task focus on the second set of problems.

Description of results: Students' ratings of task focus are shown in Figure 3. They were analyzed with a 2 (condition: training, control) x 2 (session: before train-ing, after training) analysis of variance with repeated measures on the latter factor.

FIGURE 3

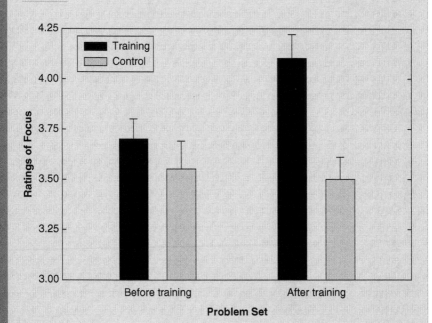

Neither the main effect for condition, $F(1, 44) = 1.15$, $\eta^2 < .01$, $p > .05$, nor the main effect for session, $F(1, 44) = 0.68$, $\eta^2 < .01$, $p > .05$, was significant. However, the interaction between these variables was significant, $F(1, 44) = 4.19$, $\eta^2 = .07$, $p < .05$. Simple effects tests revealed that ratings of task focus increased across sessions in the training condition, $F(1, 44) = 7.27$, $p < .05$, but not in the control condition, $F(1, 44) = 0.79$, $p > .05$.

2. Background: On each trial, a familiar object appeared on a computer screen for 3 seconds, followed by 2, 8, or 12 objects, with one of them the object just seen. Participants used a mouse to click on the object seen previously. Time to locate the object was recorded and averaged for sets of 2, 8, and 12 objects. The participants included younger and older adults; the hypotheses were that (a) locating the object would take less time in smaller sets, (b) older adults would need more time to locate the object, and (c) older adults would need proportionately more time to locate objects in larger sets.

    Description of results: Figure 4 depicts response times as a function of the size of the set, separately for younger and older adults. Response times were analyzed with a two-way analysis of variance in which age (younger adult, older adult) was a between-subject factor and set size (2, 8, 12 objects) was a within-subject factor. The main effect of age was significant, $F(1, 48) = 26.20$, $\eta^2 < .58$, $p < .01$, as was the main effect of set size, $F(2, 96) = 68.71$, $\eta^2 = .36$, $p < .05$. However, the interaction

(Continued)

(Continued)

FIGURE 4

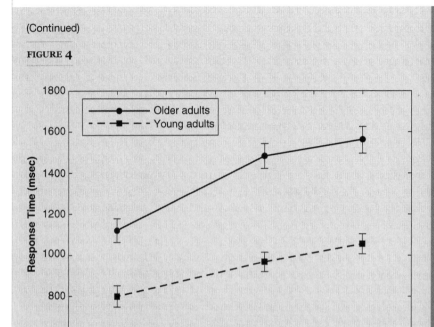

between age and set size was also significant, $F(2, 96) = 9.25$, $\eta^2 = .15$, $p < .01$. Simple effects tests revealed that the effect of set size was significant for younger adults, $F(2, 96) = 37.24$, $p < .01$, and for older adults, $F(2, 96) = 33.17$, $p < .01$.

3. *Background: College students were assigned to one of three sleep deprivation conditions: no deprivation (normal sleep), minimal deprivation (wakened once in the middle of the night), and total deprivation (not allowed to sleep at all during the night). On the following morning, participants completed a manipulation designed to make them feel relatively powerful or relatively powerless. Next, they completed a questionnaire that assessed their feelings of self-control (e.g., "I have plenty of will power") on a 7-point scale (7 = "strongly agree"). The hypothesis was that participants would report less self-control when deprived of sleep, particularly when they felt relatively powerless.

    Description of results: Students' ratings of self-control, shown in Figure 5, were analyzed with a 3 (levels of sleep deprivation) x 2 (feeling of power) analysis of variance. There was a significant main effect for level of sleep deprivation $F(2, 57) = 10.42$, $\eta^2 < .38$, $p < .01$, as well as a significant main effect of feelings of power, $F(1, 57) = 4.65$, $\eta^2 = .12$, $p < .05$. Also, the interaction between sleep deprivation and feeling of power was significant, $F(2, 57) = 3.75$, $\eta^2 = .08$, $p < .05$. Simple effects tests revealed that the effect of feeling of power was significant only in the total deprivation condition, $F(1, 57) = 8.94$, $p < .01$.

FIGURE 5

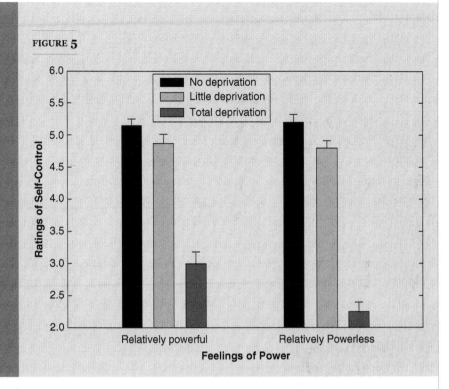

Findings From Correlational Research

In correlational research, hypotheses usually concern relations between and among variables. Such hypotheses are often tested by determining whether correlation coefficients differ significantly from o. For example, imagine a study in which we're interested in the link between self-control and antisocial behavior. We hypothesize that greater self-control is associated with less antisocial behavior. In other words, these variables should be correlated negatively. We measure these variables along with intelligence and socioeconomic status (because of the possibility that these latter two variables may covary with antisocial behavior). The results of the study are shown in Table 5, on page 85.

A description of these findings in statisticalese appears in passage 4a:

(4a)   Correlations between the four variables are shown in Table 5. Self-control was correlated significantly with verbal intelligence ($r = .23$, $p < .05$) and antisocial behavior ($r = -.37$, $p < .01$). Verbal intelligence was correlated significantly with socioeconomic status ($r = .28$, $p < .05$) and antisocial behavior ($r = -.24$, $p < .05$). Socioeconomic status was not correlated with either self-control ($r = .05$) or antisocial behavior ($r = -.07$).

This passage has several problems. First, it repeats most of the information in the table, a practice that makes one wonder why the author included the table. Second, the description is statistics oriented—focusing solely on whether correlations were significant—but doesn't tell the reader how variables were related. Said differently, the description emphasizes the size of each correlation but not its sign (i.e., whether it's positive or negative). Third, the passage ignores the hypotheses and the reasons why variables were included in the study. The critical correlation is between self-control and antisocial behavior; the others were computed simply to be sure the correlation between self-control and antisocial behavior does not reflect the impact of a third variable.

Passage 4b describes the same correlations but in a storytelling mode:

(4b)   Correlations between the four variables are shown in Table 5. As predicted, greater self-control was associated with less antisocial behavior. This relation may reflect the impact of intelligence because greater intelligence was associated with greater self-control and less antisocial behavior. However, socioeconomic status is not implicated in the link between self-control and antisocial behavior because it was unrelated to either of these variables.

Passage 4b begins with the critical correlation but emphasizes the relation between the variables, not the fact that the correlation is significant. The rest of the paragraph examines the roles intelligence and socioeconomic status might play in this relation.

In passage 4b, the description is variable oriented; passage 4c describes the same correlations but in terms of people's behaviors and traits:

(4c)   Correlations between the four variables are shown in Table 5. As predicted, individuals with greater self-control were less likely to behave antisocially. This relation may reflect the impact of intelligence because more intelligent people had greater self-control and were less likely to behave antisocially. However, socioeconomic status is not implicated in the link between self-control and antisocial behavior because people's socioeconomic status was unrelated to their self-control or their tendency to behave antisocially.

A person-oriented description is rooted in concrete behaviors and traits, making it clearer than a more abstract variable-oriented description. But sometimes behavioral descriptions get long and clumsy; "to behave antisocially" in passage 4c comes to mind. In this case the variable-oriented description may be more effective. But be consistent; don't mix the two modes.

EXERCISE 6.3

Rewrite these passages so they are story oriented, not statistics oriented.

1. Background: First-grade students in the United States and Spain were administered three tasks: (1) a measure of nonverbal intelligence, (2) a measure of their knowledge of letters and the sounds associated with them, and (3) a measure of their ability to read individual words correctly aloud. The hypothesis is that knowledge of letters will predict students' reading skill, for students in the United States and Spain, but that nonverbal intelligence will not predict reading skill.

    Description of results: Correlations between measures are shown in Table 8.[2] Language was unrelated to nonverbal intelligence, letter knowledge, or reading skill (rs = .03, –.21, and .18, respectively). Nonverbal intelligence was unrelated to letter knowledge and reading skill (rs = .19 and .15, respectively). However, letter knowledge was related to reading skill (r = .72, p < .01).

TABLE **8**   **Bivariate Correlations**

Measure	1	2	3
1. Language	–		
2. Nonverbal intelligence	.03	–	
3. Letter knowledge	–.21	.19	–
4. Reading skill	.18	.15	.72**

Note: Spanish is dummy coded as 1; English as 0.

** p < .01.

2. Background: Older adults were asked about their level of education, age, and marital status. In addition, they were asked to rate whether they were satisfied

---

[2] In the correlation matrices for Exercise 6.3, for simplicity I've omitted means and standard deviations. In practice these should always be included in a correlation matrix.

(Continued)

(Continued)

with the amount of support they received from other people. Finally, they were asked to report the frequency with which they had experienced symptoms of anxiety or depression within the past month. The hypothesis was that people who were more satisfied with their social support would be less likely to experience symptoms associated with anxiety and depression.

Description of results: Correlations between measures are shown in Table 9. Education and age were unrelated to the other measures ($rs = -.12$ to .05 for education and $-.12$ to .08 for age). Marital status was related only to mental health symptoms ($r = -.15$, $p < .05$). Perceived support was related only to mental health symptoms ($r = -.36$, $p < .01$).

TABLE 9   **Bivariate Correlations**

Measure	1	2	3	4
1. Education	–			
2. Age	−.12	–		
3. Marital status	.05	−.12	–	
4. Perceived support	−.08	.05	−.01	–
5. Mental health symptoms	−.06	.08	−.15*	−.36**

Note: Married or cohabitating is dummy coded as 1; otherwise 0.

*$p < .05$, **$p < .01$.

3.   *Background: Employees at a midsized accounting firm in Germany were asked to complete four questionnaires. One measured the employee's view that incoming e-mails were disruptive and made it difficult to complete work-related tasks. A second measured the employee's view that he or she was under pressure to complete many tasks in a limited amount of time. A third measured the employee's negative mood (e.g., being irritated or anxious), and a fourth measured the employee's positive mood (e.g., being excited or inspired). The hypothesis was that perception of e-mails as being disruptive would be associated with perception of greater time pressure and greater negative mood but would be unrelated to positive mood.

Description of results: Correlations between measures are shown in Table 10. Perception of e-mails as being disruptive was associated positively with perception of time pressure ($r = .51$, $p < .01$) and with negative mood ($r = .27$, $p < .01$) but was unrelated to positive mood ($r = .02$). Perception of time pressure was associated positively with negative mood ($r = .31$, $p < .01$) but was unrelated to positive mood ($r = -.02$). Negative mood was associated negatively with positive mood ($r = -.22$, $p < .01$).

TABLE 10 **Bivariate Correlations**

Measure	1	2	3
1. Perceived e-mails as disruptive	–		
2. Perceived time pressure	.51**	–	
3. Negative mood	.27**	.31**	–
4. Positive mood	.02	–.02	–.22**

** $p < .01$.

Correlations such as those in Tables 5 and 9 often are the starting point for more precise tests of hypotheses using sophisticated techniques such as multiple regression, structural equation modeling, and hierarchical linear modeling. In reporting findings from these kinds of analyses, you'll need to report some details because these methods are more complicated, offer many options, and are less familiar to readers. Nevertheless, stick to storytelling as much as possible. For example, Table 11 on page 98 depicts the results of multiple regression analysis of the correlations shown in Table 9. The description of these results in passage 5a emphasizes method:

(5a) The results for a hierarchical multiple regression predicting mental health symptoms are shown in Table 11. In the first step, we entered the control variables. Collectively, they accounted for 5% of the variance, but only marital status was a significant predictor ($\beta = -.10$, $p < .05$). In the second step, we entered perceived social support. This produced a significant increase in variance explained ($\Delta R^2 = .16$), and perceived social support was a significant predictor ($\beta = -.40$, $p < .01$).

The emphasis on analysis is evident in the description of the steps of the analysis and in the reporting of statistics from the table in the text. In contrast, passage 5b puts the findings in the foreground and says little about the analyses per se.

(5b) The results for a hierarchical multiple regression predicting mental health symptoms are shown in Table 11. As predicted, perceived social support predicted mental health symptoms even after controlling for education, age, and marital status.

TABLE 11   **Hierarchical Regression Analysis Predicting Mental Health Symptoms**

Predictor	Step 1	Step 2
Education	−.04	−.02
Age	.03	.05
Marital status	−.10*	−.08
Mental health symptoms		−.40**
R^2	.05*	.21**
ΔR^2	.05	.16

Note: All coefficients are standardized.

*$p < .05$. **$p < .01$.

Although the first sentence of passage 5b specifies the kind of analysis, the second sentence emphasizes the results and their fit with the study's hypothesis. This lean reporting works because hierarchical regression is relatively common. But if you report results of more complex and less familiar analyses, you may need to resort to the style of passage 5a.

ASSEMBLING THE PIECES

After you've described the key findings, you may need to describe other ancillary results. For example, when the dependent variable is the time for participants to respond, you may report analyses on the accuracy of those responses. Or in an experiment that includes a manipulation designed to induce temporary states in participants (e.g., feelings of sadness, power, or hunger), you may report analyses showing that the manipulation worked. Describe these analyses briefly, in storytelling mode. For example, sentence 6 documents that a manipulation designed to induce anger was effective:

(6)   Analyses of participants' mood before they interacted with the confederate showed that participants reported greater anger when they had been insulted by the experimenter ($M = 5.6$, $s = 1.2$) than when they had not ($M = 2.2$, $s = 0.9$), $F(1, 32) = 16.21$, $\eta^2 = .18$.

With the primary and ancillary analyses described, you can piece everything together. I recommend you begin with the ancillary findings and then move to the main results. Just as a concert starts with warm-up acts and ends with the main act, it's always better to build momentum and end strong.

I suggest you describe this organization in a brief paragraph at the beginning of the Results section. (And you could insert subheadings later in the section that identify the different analyses.)

This paragraph also allows you to describe information you don't want to repeat over and over. For example, rather than repeat "$p < .05$" dozens of times, you could include the phrase, "For effects described as significant, $p < .05$." Similarly, there may be effects of interest that were never significant in any analyses. Rather than say so repeatedly, say it once in this paragraph: "In the analyses reported here, the effect of X was never significant." Passage 7 illustrates this sort of introductory paragraph:

(7)   Results

The results are reported in two sections—one devoted to analyses of the structure of the emotion tasks and another devoted to links between performance on those tasks and participants' sense of agency. Preliminary analyses revealed comparable performance for males and females; consequently, this variable is not discussed further. Unless noted to the contrary, for all effects described as significant, $p < .01$.

A final note: Some writers are nervous about reporting their results in the economical manner I've described here. They fear reviewers may find fault with this lean style of reporting. Fortunately, there's an easy solution that can satisfy the needs of reviewers and some readers for details of analyses and the needs of most readers for a strong story line that doesn't run aground in a sea of ANOVAs. Write the Results in storytelling mode, but prepare a supplementary document that includes all the details (e.g., complete ANOVA summary tables). Most journals are happy to make such information available to reviewers and to publish it online if the article is accepted. Thus, the details are available to those who want them but don't disrupt the flow for everyone else.

WRAP-UP

1. Identify the key findings of your work—the ones worth reporting to the scientific community—and decide whether they are best depicted in a graph or a table.

2. Describe each primary outcome briefly, telling a story with a minimal amount of statistical detail.

3. Begin the Results section with a brief orienting paragraph, include ancillary analyses, and end with the main findings (saving the best for last).

FOR PRACTICE

1. Look for graphs and tables; decide whether each is the appropriate format for reporting the data.

2. Find Results sections that are written in statisticalese; rewrite in storytelling mode.

3. Look for Results sections that lead with the main findings and end with the ancillary findings. Do these seem to end with a whimper instead of a bang?

ANSWERS TO EXERCISES

Exercise 6.1

1. For this sort of study, it's important to see whether adolescents in the two conditions consume similar amounts of soda before the intervention and to see how they differ after the intervention. In other words, it's the pattern of consumption across measurements that matters. Consequently, a graph is the way to go.

    In Figure 6 on page 101, it's clear that adolescents in the two groups drank the same amount of soda before the intervention and that the intervention cut consumption in half. At 3 months after the intervention, consumption was still down from the original level, but 6 months later the benefits of the intervention had vanished. (Notice, also, that this figure includes bars depicting the 95% confidence interval around the mean.)

2. This study includes three dependent variables that can be presented easily in a table.

TABLE 12   **Descriptive Statistics**

Dependent Variable	Included Participants	Rejected Participants
Percentage displaying negative emotion	18	85
Mean ratings of sadness (SD)[a]	2.5 (1.23)	5.6 (0.91)
Percentage willing to participate in another study	78	15

[a]On a scale of 1–7 where 7 = very sad.

FIGURE 6

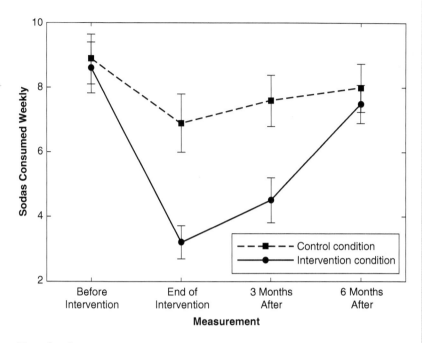

Exercise 6.2

1. Students' ratings of task focus are shown in Figure 3. Overall, students in the training and control conditions rated their focus similarly, $F(1, 44) = 1.15$, $\eta^2 < .01$, and their ratings did not change across problem sets, $F(1, 44) = 0.68$, $\eta^2 < .01$. However, the predicted interaction was significant: $F(1, 44) = 4.19$, $\eta^2 = .07$. Students who learned tips to control their attention reported greater focus, $F(1, 44) = 7.27$, in the second session (after training), but students who learned tips to control their weight did not, $F(1, 44) < 1$.[3]

2. Figure 4 depicts response times as a function of the size of the set, separately for younger and older adults. As expected, older adults took more time to respond than younger adults, $F(1, 48) = 26.20$, $\eta^2 < .58$, and both groups took more time to respond on larger sets, $F(2, 96) = 68.71$, $\eta^2 = .36$. Of particular importance was the predicted interaction between age and size of the search set, $F(2, 96) = 9.25$, $\eta^2 = .15$. Although both groups took longer to respond on larger sets, $Fs(2, 96) \geq 33.17$, the increase was greater for older adults.

---

[3] An F ratio that is less than 1 is never statistically significant, regardless of df or p. So reporting exact values for these Fs just adds a meaningless detail.

Exercise 6.3

1. Correlations between measures are shown in Table 8. As hypothesized, letter knowledge predicted reading skill, but nonverbal intelligence did not. Also as predicted, the language of instruction was unrelated to outcomes. OR

    Correlations between measures are shown in Table 8. As hypothesized, children with greater letter knowledge read more skillfully, but children with greater nonverbal intelligence did not. Also as predicted, the language children learned was unrelated to their performance on the other three tasks.

2. Correlations between measures are shown in Table 9. As predicted, greater perceived support was associated with fewer mental health symptoms. Being married or cohabitating was also associated with fewer mental health symptoms. However, this did not mediate the link between greater support and mental health because being married or cohabitating was not associated with greater support. OR

    Correlations between measures are shown in Table 9. As predicted, individuals who perceived greater support reported fewer mental health symptoms. Individuals who were married or cohabitating also reported fewer mental health symptoms. However, this did not mediate the link between greater support and mental health because individuals who were married or cohabitating were not more satisfied with social support.

7

Discussing Your Findings

Having completed an Introduction and a Results section, you can turn your attention to the Discussion. This section has a simple purpose: to consider the issues raised in the Introduction in light of the results of your work. In other words, your study was designed to provide answers to questions; here is where you explain those answers to your readers, where you tell readers what the findings mean. Writers often struggle with this section, in part because it lacks a well-defined structure. In this last lesson, we start by looking at some problems commonly encountered in Discussion sections, consider some solutions to those problems, and examine ways to end a manuscript persuasively.

SOME COMMON MISTAKES

Let's start with a six-pack of problems common to Discussion sections.

- *Too long:* Some authors feel compelled to talk about every single result, including, for example, the unexpected, uninteresting four-way interaction that probably won't be replicated. Or they feel obligated to discuss every conceivable shortcoming in their work. Don't! The Discussion is a place to say something valuable about a few major topics, not to write ad nauseam about every topic that's even remotely related to the study.

- *Poorly organized:* Too often Discussion sections seem to be written in stream-of-consciousness mode: Ideas appear without any obvious order or relation to each other. Said differently, it's as if the author wrote one paragraph about each of five different ideas and then ordered those five paragraphs randomly. The paragraphs aren't linked together and the Discussion has no overall plan.

- *Doesn't discuss:* Some authors fill the Discussion with a detailed review of the results but don't actually discuss them. A brief summary of key findings is an excellent way to begin a Discussion, but then you need to put those findings in perspective for the reader, explaining what conclusions they warrant and what questions remain unanswered.

- *Off topic:* Scientists often have opinions about a general area of research, and they sometimes use the Discussion to get these thoughts "off their chest"—even when they're only remotely related to the study being reported. Of course, if your findings have broader implications for the field, feel free to mention them. But having written six solid paragraphs on relevant topics does not give you license to go off topic in the seventh paragraph.

- *Inconsistent or inappropriate tone:* In Lesson 2 we considered the importance of writing in a voice that balances hedges and intensifiers so that your writing seems self-assured without seeming arrogant. Nowhere is this more important than in the Discussion. As you describe how your findings address the issues that motivated the study, you don't want to seem too pushy or too dismissive of other relevant work. Yet you shouldn't be overly cautious—hedging everything—because readers won't believe your conclusions if you don't seem to believe them yourself! To achieve the desired cautiously confident voice, use the strategy described in Lesson 2: Write a draft without any hedges or intensifiers, then add hedges and intensifiers as needed, with more of the former than the latter.

- *Too much self-praise:* Too often authors fill their Discussion with phrases such as "We are the first to show . . ." or "These findings are important because . . ." It's as if the author doubts the reader will believe the findings are sufficiently innovative or important and resorts to these phrases to convince the reader of the study's value. The place to make the case for a study is in the Introduction: A clear and compelling rationale for the study should make it obvious how the work is innovative and

EXERCISE 7.1

A good organization won't eliminate the problem of self-praise in a Discussion, so you need to be able to recognize such writing and purge it. Which of the following sentences seem guilty of self-praise?

1. These findings support the hypothesis that children prefer in-groups as soon as they can distinguish them from out-groups.
2. The results reported here are rich in their implications for the literature on meta-cognition.
3. This study is the first attempt to determine whether the absence of green space in a person's environment is linked to symptoms of anxiety and depression.
4. Our findings complement those of laboratory studies in showing that diverse groups are sometimes less productive.
5. Other research has shown the effect of context on decision-making; the ground-breaking contribution of the present experiment is in demonstrating that this effect is a by-product of basic cognitive processes.
6. This finding is particularly valuable in suggesting that discrete emotions are rooted in feelings of arousal.

valuable; you needn't waste words reminding the reader that "we're first!"[1] or trying to convince the reader "This really is important!"

Except for self-praise, these problems stem from the lack of a well-defined structure for the Discussion. An effective plan to guide your writing usually eliminates problems of length, organization, and inappropriate topics. The next section provides a handy template for writing a Discussion.

A TEMPLATE FOR A SUCCESSFUL DISCUSSION SECTION

You can avoid many of the problems that plague Discussion sections by using the template shown in Table 13. Because the structure of a Discussion section can vary depending on the study, begin this section with a brief orienting paragraph. It should contain one to three sentences in which you review the key findings of your work; if you have more than three sentences, you're probably going into too much detail. Then include one or two sentences in which you provide an overview of the rest of the Discussion, an overview that's linked to the subheadings used in the rest of the Discussion. Passage 1 shows an illustrative orienting paragraph.

---

[1] After all, not many authors write, "We're the 64th group to show this effect." Except for replication studies, most studies are the first of their kind, so this is better left unsaid.

TABLE 13   **A Template for a Discussion Section**

Section	Purpose
Introductory paragraph	Provides a brief summary of the findings and an overview of the rest of the Discussion
Limiting conditions	Describes features of the study that limit the conclusions that can be drawn
Study-specific issues, 1–3	Discusses the issues central to the study (at least one, no more than three) as well as unexpected but provocative findings
Implications for X	Discusses the implications of the findings for social policy, treatment, or instruction
General implications	Links the findings to more general concerns and issues associated with the area of research

(1)   Both studies reported here demonstrate that parents—particularly fathers—report greater happiness than nonparents. This was the case in Study 1 for a convenience sample in which participants provided multiple reports of happiness daily and in Study 2 for a nationally representative sample in which participants estimated their overall happiness. In the remainder of this Discussion, we discuss some limiting conditions on this evidence and then consider some differences between our findings and prior work on parents' happiness.

This orienting paragraph leads the reader to expect two main sections, one on limiting conditions and one on differences between the present and prior findings, each introduced with a subheading.

The orienting paragraph is then followed by several elements, each introduced with a subheading.

- *Limiting conditions:* Start by considering the features of the research that may limit the conclusions able to be drawn from the findings. This is not "confession" time where you list each blemish in your work. Nor is it the place to rationalize weak data or serious flaws. (If your work has unconvincing data or fatal flaws, don't try to rescue the work in the Discussion; do a better study.) Instead, mention reasons why your work is not the "last word" on the topic. Passage 2 illustrates this kind of paragraph (based on the study described in passage 10 of Lesson 5, on page 78).

(2)   Two features of this work limit the conclusions we can draw about developmental change in the structure of executive function. First,

the study was cross-sectional, not longitudinal, and thus is subject to all the shortcomings associated with the former design. Second, although we measured the components of executive function with commonly used tasks, researchers disagree on the tasks that best tap into inhibition, shifting, and updating (e.g., Tremblay & Flores, 2012). Whether other plausible measures of executive function would yield comparable results is an open question.

- *Study-specific issues:* Next discuss one to three issues specific to the study. Most of these will be linked to the rationale for the study. This is your chance to explain how your findings yield greater understanding of the phenomena that motivated your work. Of course, sometimes studies yield unanticipated but provocative findings; these could be examined under one of the study-specific headings. Passage 3 illustrates a paragraph dealing with an issue from the study mentioned in passage 1 on page 105–106.

(3)   Our findings contrast with some reports in the literature in which parenting has been associated with relatively less happiness (e.g., Levine, 1972). Our view is that these differences are more apparent than real and hinge on the choice of the reference point. Some of these studies (e.g., Campbell & Harris, 2008) have examined changes in parents' happiness as their children develop and have found that parents are less happy when their children are infants. Others (e.g., Vejcek, Dikstra, & Karlsson, 2013) have examined changes in parents' happiness as a function of the nature of their activities and have found that parents report being happier when involved in activities that do not include their children. However, such life span- and activity-related variations in parents' happiness are not inconsistent with parents' overall level of happiness being greater than that of nonparents.

- *Implications for . . .* Often findings from research have implications for social policy, treatment, or instruction. Use this section to explain the impact of your findings on, for example, policies toward military families or treatment for people with depression. Passage 4 shows part of a paragraph dealing with the implications of findings for teaching children how to spell.

(4)   The present findings also have implications for how elementary schoolchildren are taught to spell. In the United States, spelling instruction often revolves around lists of words that children

memorize. Such instruction is sometimes supplemented with phonics instruction: for example, teaching children that when a one-syllable word ends in *e*, the prior vowel "says its name" (as in *kale*). However, the present findings imply that children could benefit from learning about links between morphology and spelling. For example, they could learn that although the past tense of many verbs sounds as if it ends in *t* (e.g., *dressed*, *laughed*, *helped*), the ending is spelled *–ed*.

- *General implications:* Link the study to more general concerns in the area of research. This is your opportunity to show how your work is relevant to a broader range of issues and thus is of interest to more than a handful of experts. For example, the authors of the study described in passage 1 might link their findings to other topics in the study of parents' emotions or parents' well-being. Passage 5 illustrates the beginning of a paragraph discussing the implications of the study cited in passage 10 of Lesson 5 and passage 2 of this lesson:

(5)   More generally, the present findings contribute to a more nuanced view of the processes that drive cognitive development during childhood. Specifically, cognitive development is often viewed as the by-product of general processes like executive function as well as domain-specific processes (McMillin & Fricker, 2009). Yet we know little about interactions between these two sources of cognitive growth. Given the present findings of qualitative and quantitative change in executive function during childhood, discovering these interactions will require . . .

This paragraph takes a step back and examines the findings concerning developmental change in executive function from the broader perspective of other factors that contribute to cognitive growth in childhood.

The elements of this template provide a starting point you can tailor to suit the needs of your paper. If you're reporting a simple, straightforward study, a five-paragraph Discussion might be perfectly adequate—one paragraph each for orientation, limiting conditions, two issues, and implications. If, instead, you're reporting a half dozen experiments, you might begin the Discussion with a paragraph titled "Summary of Findings." And not every study will have implications for social policy, treatment, or instruction, so that section could be deleted. The point is simple: Make the template your own, adjusting it to fit each manuscript that you write.

EXERCISE 7.2

Find a published article in which the Discussion lacks subheadings. Identify the function of each paragraph—summary of findings and overview, limiting conditions, study-specific issues, and general implications. Are there paragraphs that have other functions? If the Discussion doesn't have an orienting paragraph, write one.

EXERCISE 7.3

For each of the studies described in Exercise 5.4 on pages 70–80, identify one limiting condition that could be described, as well as one study-specific issue.

Regardless of the variations you introduce, by starting with this template, you'll avoid the first four common problems listed on pages 103–105. The template provides focus and structure so that the Discussion won't be too long but will be organized, discuss the issues at hand, and stay on topic.

Finally, two features of this template may seem at odds with research reports you've read. First, some authors discuss limiting conditions toward the end of the Discussion, but I think that's less effective. The rule that sentences should end strong applies to the Discussion section as a whole. Get the limiting conditions out of the way and then move to the provocative aspects of your work, building momentum as you go. Second, there is no section titled "Directions for Future Research." Of course, you should point to the kinds of studies needed, but those recommendations are more compelling when they appear in the context of specific, unanswered questions. For example, if the authors of passage 3 wanted to suggest the kind of study that would test their explanation of the difference between their results and previous findings, that suggestion is more constructive if presented with their explanation instead of in a separate section.

ENDING STRONG

Your paper needs to end with a bang, not a whimper. Avoid banal endings like those in sentences 6 and 7 that simply call for more research:

(6)   Future research on this phenomenon is essential.

(7)   Answering these lingering questions is a topic for future research.

These sentences apply to 99% of all research so they add nothing meaningful. Instead, aim for a memorable ending whose take-home message makes readers believe the time spent on your article was well invested.

A first step in writing a strong ending is identifying the take-home message and a vivid way of conveying it. Often the solution is readily available: the hook you used to grab the reader's attention in the Introduction. Lesson 5 mentions several ways to get readers to sit up and take notice: an interesting slice of behavior, a rhetorical question, an intriguing statistic or an anecdote. These hooks often can be the basis for a powerful ending. In fact, you should select a hook in the first place based, in part, on its value in setting up a strong ending. For example, Lesson 5 included these four examples of behavior, rhetorical questions, interesting statistics, and anecdotes as hooks:

(8)   When people enter a building, others often hold the door for them. Although such interactions are commonplace, we know little about forms of social interaction like these that involve physical cooperation.

(9)   Suppose you want to buy a new camera. Would you prefer to shop at a store that has three cameras in your price range or a store that has 12? Research on choice overload suggests you will prefer the store with more choices but be less satisfied with a camera purchased there (Harris, Becker, & Hall, 2010).

(10)   Less than 10% of the world's population reads English, yet 90% of the published articles on reading have involved English-speaking readers (Olsen & Nagy, 2012); this is potentially problematic because English is an unusual language in that spellings and sounds are not linked consistently (Moreau, Horvat, Mertens, & Gruber, 2008).

(11)   In 1949, 16 firefighters were on the verge of being trapped by a forest fire. One of them, Wagner Dodge, unexpectedly realized that by setting a small, controllable fire, he could clear a path for him and his coworkers to escape. Dodge's solution illustrates an "aha experience"—a solution to a problem that occurs suddenly and effortlessly (Posselt & Krupa, 2018).

The starting point for a strong ending is to return to the hook, updating it in light of what your findings reveal. For example, suppose the study mentioned in passage 8 showed that people hold a door longer when two people are following them than when just one follows. Sentence 12a shows an ending that highlights the take-home message by citing the hook from the Introduction:

(12a) Thus, the present findings highlight the role of shared effort in driving physical cooperation, and they lead to some practical advice: If you want the door held for you as you enter a building, arrive with a friend, not alone.

Sentence 13 illustrates use of the hook from passage 9:

(13)   The work reported here confirms that choice overload affects evaluation of luxury goods just as it affects evaluations of trinkets used in most previous work. And the results lead to a strong recommendation for consumers: You'll be happier with your new camera (or car or fancy watch) if you just consider a few of the models that fit your needs, not all of them.

To underscore the conclusions you want readers to take away from your paper, consider the techniques for emphasis mentioned in Lesson 2: using *it*, *there*, and *what* to shift text to the end of the sentence and *not only X but Y* to highlight new findings. For example, a manuscript's end is a great place to use *what*, as illustrated in sentence 12b.

(12b)   Thus, what stands out in this work is the role of shared effort in driving physical cooperation; and the work leads to some practical advice . . .

If previous findings had implicated internal models of action in physical cooperation but the new findings implicate shared effort, then you could use *not only X but Y* as in sentence 12c:

(12c)   Thus, the present findings indicate that not only internal models of action but shared effort drive physical cooperation; and the findings lead to some practical advice . . .

EXERCISE 7.4

Use the hooks you created in Exercise 5.1 (or the ones I suggested on page 81) to write a paper-ending sentence. For the first study, assume that negative events were recalled more accurately than positive ones. For the second study, assume that heterogeneous groups were shown to be more difficult to form and more challenging to manage (results that replicate prior findings) and less productive than homogeneous groups (a novel result). For the third study, assume that wellness programs were effective when they rewarded people for healthy behavior instead of punishing them. For the fourth study, assume the endorsements by celebrities were more effective when celebrities were familiar and credible but that their trustworthiness had no impact.

You could even combine *what* with *not only X but Y* as in passage 12d:

(12d) Thus, what stands out in the present work is that not only internal models of action but shared effort drive physical cooperation; and the findings lead to some practical advice . . .

One other useful tool for emphasizing your take-home message is the *periodic sentence*. I didn't mention this kind of sentence earlier because periodic sentences can be so over the top that they aren't appropriate for routine emphasis. But they can be a wonderful way to end a paper.

Periodic sentences have two essential components. The first is an introductory clause that's much longer than average—exactly the kind of clause that Lesson 1 urges you to eliminate. The second defining element is a word that's repeated, sometimes several times, in the introductory clause. Passage 14 illustrates a famous periodic sentence:

(14)   With malice toward none; with charity for all; with firmness in the right . . . let us strive on to finish the work we are in [and] to bind up the nation's wounds.

This sentence, taken from Abraham Lincoln's second inaugural address, begins with a long introductory clause in which *with* is repeated three times; both the length of the clause and the repeated *with* get the reader's attention.

In a Discussion section, a periodic sentence is a great way to summarize your evidence and restate the critical conclusion. That is, you present the evidence in the long introductory clause and the conclusion in the briefer main clause, as in sentence 15:

(15)   Given that children who read normally typically have greater phonological awareness than do children with reading impairments, given that children's phonological awareness predicts their reading skill later in development, and given that children's reading improves after training in phonological awareness, we conclude that phonological awareness is an essential prerequisite for mastering reading.

The 40-word introductory clause summarizes the evidence, introducing each finding with *given*; the 12-word main clause provides the conclusion that follows from that evidence. Periodic sentences could also be built around repetition of *because*, *when*, or *considering*, with each introducing a piece of evidence that supports the conclusion.

EXERCISE 7.5

Use techniques for emphasis and spicy writing to improve the conclusions you wrote for Exercise 7.4.

Finally, if you want to pull out all the stops, this is a great place to spice up your writing as described in the second part of Lesson 3. Figures of speech (e.g., metaphor, antimetabole) and neologisms capture the reader's attention wherever they appear, a feature that makes them especially well-suited to end your Discussion. For example, sentence 16 illustrates use of antimetabole to highlight findings from work on training aggressive adolescents to recognize facial emotions:

(16)   When aggressive adolescents recognize anger in a face, they are better able to face their own anger.

And sentence 17 shows how a new word created by adding a suffix can punch up a conclusion:

(17)   What stands out in each study is that boys and girls are equally likely to excel on math problems; thus, boys and girls are equally capable of becoming mathaholics.

By combining these techniques for spiced-up writing with the hook from the Introduction and techniques for emphasis, you can end your paper on a high note. This ending—along with a goose-bump-inducing Introduction and a Results section with a strong story line—is likely to make readers believe your article is exceptional and well worth reading.

WRAP-UP

1.   Avoid common problems of Discussion sections, which include being too long and poorly organized, rehashing but not discussing results, wandering off topic, using an inappropriate tone, and indulging in self-praise.

2.   A useful organization for a Discussion section begins with an orienting paragraph (review of findings and overview of the rest of the section), followed by sections devoted to limiting conditions, a few study-specific issues, and general implications.

3.   End strong by applying techniques for emphasis.

FOR PRACTICE

1. Scan the Discussion section of several articles for the six common problems described on pages 103–105.

2. Find an article in which the Discussion section has no headings; revise the text using the template provided in this chapter.

3. Find an article that ends in a whimper. Revise it to provide the bang.

ANSWERS TO EXERCISES

Exercise 7.1

The following sentences have self-praise (in italics).

1. The *results reported here are rich* in their implications for the literature on metacognition.

2. This study is the *first attempt* to determine whether the absence of green space in a person's environment is linked to symptoms of anxiety and depression.

3. Other research has shown the effect of context on decision-making; the *groundbreaking contribution of the present experiment* is in demonstrating that this effect is a by-product of basic cognitive processes.

4. This finding *is particularly valuable* in suggesting that discrete emotions are rooted in feelings of arousal.

Exercise 7.3

Study 1: One limiting condition would be the possibility that the positive and negative emotions associated with winning and losing in sports may not compare with those of other kinds of events (e.g., the joy of a wedding vs. the sadness of a divorce). A study-specific issue would be the mechanisms that make negative events more memorable than positive events.

Study 2: One limiting condition would be the use of college students; would the finding hold for the population at large? The most important study-specific issue would concern links among stress, negative affect, and depressive symptoms.

Exercise 7.4

1. The present findings suggest that the agony of defeat is more memorable than the thrill of victory because people remembered features of losses more accurately than features of wins.

2. Based on the present work, if you want to be a productive scientist, you should join a relatively homogeneous group because heterogeneous groups were more difficult to form, more challenging to manage, and less productive.

3. Consequently, the results reported here show how U.S. companies can save some of the $3,000 they lose annually due to cost of health care, absenteeism, and reduced productivity: Companies can embrace wellness programs that reward employees for healthy behavior because such programs result in lower costs of health care, less absenteeism, and greater productivity.

Exercise 7.5

1. What emerges consistently in this work is that negative events are remembered more accurately than positive ones: For sports fans, the memories you lose over time are not the memories of when you lose.

2. Thus, given the evidence that heterogeneous groups are not only more difficult to form and more challenging to manage but are less productive, if you want to have a publish-but-not-perish career, you should join a relatively homogeneous group.

3. Consequently, the results reported here show how U.S. companies can save some of the $3,000 they lose annually due to cost of health care, absenteeism, and reduced productivity: Companies can embrace wellness programs that reward employees for healthy behavior because such programs result in not only lower costs of health care and less absenteeism but greater productivity.

Epilogue: Writing a Title, Abstract, and Method Section

Lessons 5 through 7 focused on the three parts of a manuscript—Introduction, Results, and Discussion—that determine how readers evaluate your work. Based on what you say in these sections, reviewers may recommend that your manuscript be accepted for publication or rejected. In contrast, the title, abstract, and Method section have relatively little impact on the fate of your manuscript in scientific review. Reviewers sometimes may ask authors to clarify methods or suggest another title, but I can't recall a reviewer *ever* writing, "This paper should be rejected because it has a lousy title" or "This paper should be accepted because the Method section is written so well."

Most books that introduce students to APA style have basic information about how to write a title, abstract, and Method section; frankly, there's not much left to say. So what follows are a few suggestions for writing these elements of your manuscript, along with a manuscript that illustrates many of the tips described in Lessons 1–7.

THE TITLE

A title matters. It is the first part of your article a reader sees, and it's how articles are retrieved by Internet search engines. So, it's worth spending time to create a title that conveys your work accurately. I suggest you avoid several genres of titles:

- *Titles that are too cute or too clever:* Authors sometimes include the names of songs, television programs, or events from popular culture in their titles, usually followed by a more scientific-sounding phrase.

The problem with this approach is that popular culture varies across geography and time. What may be a great example of popular culture in one country may be meaningless in another country and meaningless everywhere in a decade or so.[1] If you want to engage the reader with a nonscientific phrase, proverbs (e.g., *A bird in the hand is better than two in the bush*) represent a better choice because they have, by definition, proven the test of time and, in many cases, are common across cultures.

- *Titles that include "preliminary":* Some authors apparently think that adding "preliminary" may convince editors and reviewers to use a lower bar for evaluating a manuscript. I'm skeptical that this works. If a study is really preliminary (e.g., the sample is too small), use the findings to design a study that actually addresses the issue at hand, but don't try to publish the preliminary findings.

- *Titles of the form "the effects of the independent variable on the dependent variable":* Undergraduates (at least in the United States) often use this kind of title for their research, so it tends to make your work seem unsophisticated. More important, psychological scientists typically are not interested in variables per se; instead, they're interested in the insights variables can provide on behavior, cognition, and affect.

Instead of these kinds of titles, I encourage titles that describe the results of your work. Here are two examples, both from my work: "Longitudinal evidence that increases in processing speed and working memory enhance children's reasoning" and "Processing time decreases globally at an exponential rate during childhood and adolescence." Both titles are succinct summaries of the main findings reported in the article.

Of course, sometimes a study's key results are too complex to be summarized neatly in a single, concise sentence. In this case, I suggest a title that mentions the key constructs from the study. Examples include "Linking emotions, social support, and health" or "The role of the medial temporal lobe in memory aging."

You don't need to spend hours perfecting a title (e.g., trying to find the ideal proverb), but it should be more than an afterthought. A good title will appeal to readers and search engines alike, increasing the impact of the work you report.

---

[1]Here's one of my titles that shows the problem: "Different Slopes for Different Folks: Process Analysis of Spatial Aptitude." The "Different Slopes for Different Folks" was based on a song by Sly and the Family Stone ("Everyday People," No. 1 on the pop charts for a week in 1969) that included the lyric "different strokes for different folks." It referred to the fact that in our research we calculated the slope of a function for each participant and then looked at how these slopes differed across participants. Understanding our title presumed familiarity with the song, which was not known universally when we published our paper and is known even less today. Bad choice— I've never done it again.

ABSTRACT

A good title grabs your reader's attention; a well-written abstract sustains it. Abstracts written in APA style usually consist of a single paragraph that includes one to two sentences about the background (or problem), hypotheses, methods, results, and conclusions. In writing the abstract,

- write two to three sentences for each of the components of the abstract (e.g., background, methods) and then use the tips in Lesson 3 to pare it down to the specified number of words;

- be sure the writing is clear and nontechnical, particularly regarding the reasons why your results represent a substantial advance in scientific understanding; and

- write it after the rest of the manuscript is finished, so you know what the paper actually says!

METHOD

A Method section describes how you conducted the study, in sufficient detail such that others could replicate your work. Writing a Method section is straightforward and all about details, with little room for creativity or the rhetorical devices described earlier in this book. For that reason, I usually turn to the Method section when I'm having difficulty writing a more important part of the manuscript. As you write this section, I urge you to

- use subheadings freely, starting with the mandatory *Participants* and *Procedure* but adding others as necessary;

- avoid abbreviations and instead use descriptive terms for experimental conditions and names of variables;

- provide as much information as possible about the participants in your study (e.g., "We tested 36 college students" won't do!);

- describe what participants in the study actually did, not what they were asked to do (e.g., not "Participants were then asked to complete a questionnaire . . . " but "Participants then completed a questionnaire . . . "); and

- upload copies of all materials (e.g., stimuli, questionnaires) to the journal's website as supplementary material to be published online only.

AN ILLUSTRATIVE MANUSCRIPT

Figure 7 depicts the Introduction, Results, and Discussion sections for a hypothetical study, along with my comments explaining some of the techniques used in writing and revising.

FIGURE 7

In 2016, a teenage driver in Florida texted her boyfriend, "I can't wait to see you this weekend!" Moments later she was killed when the car she was driving left the road and struck a tree. Unfortunately, this story is all too common: Adolescent drivers often use their smartphones to call, e-mail, or text, actions that can lead to disaster. Nearly half of adolescent drivers report using cell phones while driving, and this age group has the greatest proportion of fatal crashes linked to distracted driving (National Center for Statistics and Analysis, 2017).

> The article begins with an anecdote to hook the reader. [p 70–71]

> In the first draft of the manuscript, this paragraph began with "In order to" but that phrase could be replaced with the word "To." [p 34]

> The original version of the sentence included the phrase "prevent drivers from texting while driving." In the revision, "drivers from" was dropped because readers can infer that drivers are doing the texting. [p 32]

To reduce distracted driving, many U.S. states have banned texting while driving and others have implemented public service announcements (via radio, television, and billboards) that remind drivers of the hazards of distracted driving. However, neither approach reduces distracted driving (Harding, 2013; Lennon, Rentfro, & O'Leary, 2010). Another approach is using applications for smartphones that prevent texting while driving. Such apps have promise, but some are expensive and some can be disabled by drivers (Jolly, 2016).

> The original version of the sentence included the phrase "some are not cheap" but the negative ("not cheap") was replaced with the affirmative ("expensive"). [p 31]

> In this paragraph, the topic sentence introduces the idea of stickers to remind drivers; the next two sentences provide supporting details, describing instances in which stickers have been successful reminders. [p 50–51]

Yet another approach involves using stickers placed in a car's windshield to remind drivers to pay attention. Brief reminders of this sort have sometimes succeeded in helping people to be immunized and to drink liquids to avoid dehydration (Bhatti, Ash, Gokani, & Singh, 2017; Crawford, Barfield, Hunt, Pitcher, & Buttery, 2014). In addition, stickers placed on a car's windshield reminding drivers and passengers to "buckle up" doubled use of seat belts (Thyer & Geller, 1987).

> "Reminder" is a nominalization that allows the sentence to begin with a familiar idea (i.e., it refers to the "stickers placed in a car's windshield to remind drivers to pay attention"). [p 56–57]

> In this sentence "sometimes" is a hedge, indicating that reminders can work but not always. [p 18–20]

> The original version of the sentence included the phrase "to receive immunizations." In the revision, the nominalization "immunizations" was replaced by the verb "immunized." [p 3–4]

Taking this approach, Eriksson and Metcalf (2016) found that a sticker reminding young adult drivers to pay attention resulted in less texting while driving. On the one hand, the finding is encouraging in suggesting a simple, inexpensive method for discouraging texting while driving. On the other hand, the finding is limited because the study did not include adolescent drivers, relied on self-reports of distracted driving, and did not evaluate the extended impact of reminders. Thus, the results suggest that reminder stickers have promise but more thorough evaluation is needed.

> In this sentence and the next sentence, the studies are in the background but the key ideas are in the foreground. [p 74]

> This paragraph has a contrastive structure and uses "On the one hand" with "on the other hand" to highlight the contrast between the study's contribution and what's left unknown. [p 51–52]

> The concluding sentence highlights the contrast between the contributions ("reminder stickers have promise") and the limits ("more thorough evaluation is needed"). [p 53–54]

The aim of the present study was to address some of the limits of the Eriksson and Metcalf (2016) study, thereby providing additional evidence concerning the effectiveness of stickers in reducing distracted driving. For 6 weeks, 16- to 18-year-olds drove cars fitted with dashboard cameras that recorded the drivers' behavior. At the beginning of the study, half the drivers were reminded of the dangers of distracted driving and watched as an auto instructor installed a "Drive Safely—Pay Attention" sticker in the windshield; half were reminded of the importance of regular auto maintenance as the instructor installed a "Check Oil and Water Regularly" sticker.

> This paragraph and the next wrap up the introduction and set the stage for the study. The two paragraphs follow the three parts of the suggested template, beginning with the aims, then describing methods (briefly), and ending with the expected outcomes. [p 78–79]

> In the first draft of the manuscript, the phrase was "...were reminded carefully of..." but "carefully" was an unnecessary adverb and deleted. [p 35–36]

Every two weeks, drivers completed a questionnaire assessing their beliefs on the dangers of distracted driving, and the video recordings from the dashboard cameras were downloaded. We expected drivers who were reminded to pay attention would text less often while driving and would rate such behavior as more dangerous.

Method

. . . . .

Results

The results are reported in two sections: The first describes results of analyses of observations of drivers' texting, and the second describes results of analyses of drivers' ratings of the risks of texting. These

> Notice that the predictions are phased in terms of the actual dependent variables (number of texts, ratings), not underlying constructs (distracted driving).

> This sentence provides an overview of the rest of the Results section. [p 99]

analyses are described briefly here; all details of the analyses are available in a supplementary document available online. Unless noted to the contrary, for all effects described as significant, $p < .01$. ◀······

> This sentence establishes the significance level used throughout the section so that individual p values need not be reported. [p 99]

Analyses of Observations of Texting While Driving

> This heading (and the one below it) corresponds directly to the phrasing used in describing the organization of the Results section. [p 99]

The mean number of days (out of 14) on which drivers were observed texting in each of the three 2-week periods is shown in Figure 1, separately for the two groups of drivers. As hypothesized, participants driving cars with safety-oriented stickers texted less than participants driving cars with maintenance-oriented stickers, $F(1, 38) = 8.09$, $\eta^2 = .16$. During the first 2-week period, participants with safety-oriented stickers texted half as frequently as those with maintenance-oriented stickers, but this difference dropped by the third 2-week period, $F(2, 76) = 6.32$, $\eta^2 = 14$.

> Notice that the structure of the ANOVA—2 groups x 3 2-week periods—is not mentioned. [p 89]

> This phrase reminds the reader that participants driving cars with safety-related stickers were expected to text less often. [p 89]

> The finding is described in terms of what participants did, *not* in terms of conditions ("people in the safety sticker condition texted less than those in the maintenance sticker condition") or in terms of main effects ("there was a main effect of condition. . ."). [p 89]

> The analysis of variance revealed a significant main effect of weeks (more days with texting in week 3 than in week 1) but it's not reported here because (a) it's an artifact of the interaction between group and week, (b) it's unrelated to the hypotheses that motivated the study, and (c) it's described in the supplementary document. [p 99]

Analyses of Ratings of Danger of Texting While Driving

Participants' ratings of the danger of texting for each of the three 2-week periods are shown in Figure 2, separately for the two groups of drivers. As expected, participants

FIGURE 1

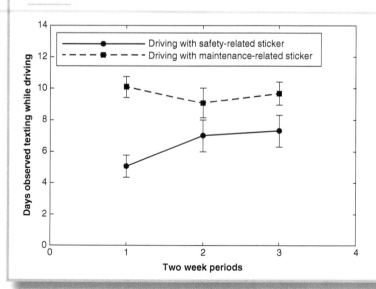

FIGURE **2**

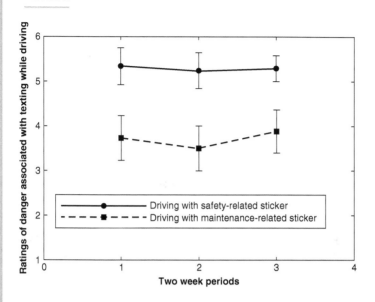

Two week periods

driving cars with safety-oriented stickers rated texting while driving as more dangerous than did participants driving cars with maintenance-oriented stickers, $F(1, 38) = 14.32$, $\eta^2 = .24$. This difference did not vary significantly over the three 2-week periods, $F < 1$.

> This paragraph tells a story about the findings, with the inferential statistics relegated to the background (i.e., the inferential statistics document the story but are not the story). [p 87]

> When F < 1, there's no need to provide the exact value. [p 101]

Discussion

> This paragraph has two parts: the first two sentences review the findings and the third sentence provides an overview of the rest of the discussion section. [p 105–106]

Compared with participants driving cars with maintenance stickers, participants driving cars with safety stickers texted less often and rated texting while driving as more dangerous. However, over the 6 weeks of the study, participants driving cars with safety stickers gradually texted more often. In the remainder of this Discussion, I consider some limiting conditions on the findings, address the gradual decline in the effectiveness of safety-related stickers, and examine the challenges of scaling up such a program to a large population.

> This sentence begins with a relatively long dependent clause, but I wanted to establish the reference point (participants driving cars with maintenance stickers) in a dependent clause so the independent clause could focus on the findings for participants driving cars with safety stickers. [p 22–23]

Limiting Conditions

The study includes two features that limit the conclusions that can be drawn. First, the study observed drivers for only 6 weeks, a feature that limits the ability to evaluate the long-term impact of safety-related stickers. This is potentially worrisome because stickers seemed to have less impact on texting toward the end of the study. Second, the sample included a relatively small number of adolescents—too few to determine whether the impact of safety stickers was the same for adolescents who had just learned to drive and those who were relatively more experienced. In addition, the study did not include young adults, an age group that texts more often than any other. Thus, conclusions from the present findings are limited to the relatively short-term impact of stickers on a broad range of adolescent drivers.

Addressing the Decline in the Effectiveness of Safety-Related Stickers

Although texting was consistently rated as dangerous, safety-related reminders became less effective over the study. Such a relapse is common in programs designed to change behavior. For example, programs that aim to stop smoking or encourage exercising are often effective in the short term (e.g., many smokers quit) but not in the long-term (e.g., smokers resume smoking). Some methods seem to be more effective in changing behavior initially, but others are effective in maintaining changed behaviors (Glanz & Bishop, 2010). For instance, programs for losing weight focus on strategies to achieve a desirable state (e.g., limiting number of calories consumed) and health care professionals monitor progress toward that state; programs for maintaining weight loss focus on strategies to keep from returning to an undesirable state (e.g., avoiding restaurants that emphasize entrees high in calories), and participants monitor their success in maintaining their weight loss (Voils et al., 2014). Such findings suggest that different methods may be needed to avoid a relapse in texting.

The original dependent clause began, ". . . which limits. . ." I replaced that with ". . .a feature that. . ." giving the sentence more direction. [p 9–10]

"Seemed to have" illustrates a hedge. [p 18]

The concluding sentence briefly mentions the two features cited in the paragraph (short-term impact only, heterogeneous adolescent drivers) in the order they appeared in the paragraph. [p 53–54]

The first version of this sentence was "Over the course of the study, drivers in cars with safety-related reminders gradually texted more often, despite believing that texting is dangerous." But the rest of the paragraph emphasizes concepts (e.g., relapse, methods, programs), not people, so the sentence was revised as this: "Over the course of the study, safety-related reminders became less effective, even though texting continued to be rated as dangerous." But that sentence ended with the data on ratings, a structure that put the emphasis on the secondary finding. In the final version of the sentence, the finding from ratings was put in an introductory clause so the sentence could end with the main finding (i.e., that safety-related reminders became less effective). [p. 22–23, 59–61]

The original version included "behavioral patterns," a phrase that conveyed nothing beyond "behavior." [p 33–34]

"Often" illustrates use of a hedge. [p 18]

The first version of this sentence was extraordinarily long: "For instance, programs for losing weight focus on strategies to achieve a desirable state (e.g., limiting number of calories consumed) and health-care professionals monitor progress toward that state but programs for maintaining weight loss focus on strategies to keep from returning to an undesirable state (e.g., avoiding restaurants that emphasize entrees high in calories) and participants monitor their success in maintaining their weight loss." In revising, I dropped the "but" and created two sentences: "For instance, programs for losing weight. . ." and "Programs for maintaining weight loss..." To highlight the link between the sentences, the final version links the sentences with a semicolon and uses parallel structure (i.e., "programs for A focus on strategies to B and C monitor their D"). [p 11–12]

Challenges of Scaling Up an Intervention

Efforts to scale up public-health interventions often encounter challenges (Richardson, 2012). For example, programs to discourage adolescents from smoking are sometimes seen as expensive and may threaten special interests (e.g., the tobacco industry). In scaling up a sticker-based safety intervention, one obvious obstacle is determining how stickers would be distributed.

> Some possibilities would be to have stickers distributed by primary-care physicians in conjunction with an adolescent's physical exam, by insurance agencies in conjunction with bills for insurance, or by government agencies in conjunction with issuing drivers' licenses.

This sentence uses parallel structure to avoid sprawl. Each phrase has the structure "...by X in conjunction with Y..." where X is an actor (physicians, insurance agencies, government agencies) and Y is when stickers would be distributed (e.g., when issuing a drivers' licenses) [p. 11].

None of these approaches is perfect. For example, many physicians are unenthusiastic about providing such public-health information during a brief appointment (Rubio-Valera et al., 2014), and many adolescents do not have regular physical exams. In addition, none of these approaches guarantees that drivers would actually install stickers.

The original version of the sentence included the phrase ". . . stickers in their car's windshield." At this point in the paper, readers know where stickers go, so that phrase was deleted. [p 32–33]

Addressing these (and other) challenges to implementation is paramount because safety stickers are potentially not only an effective but an inexpensive way to prevent the distracted driving that leads to tragedies like the one described earlier that killed the Florida teenager.

This sentence includes the "not only X but Y" construction to convey emphasis. [p 25]

The manuscript ends by connecting the findings to the anecdote used to hook the reader in the Introduction. [p 110–111]

Appendix: Submitting the Manuscript for Publication

With the writing finished, you're nearly ready to submit. But first, get feedback from a few colleagues. Be sure to ask for comments from at least one person who is not familiar with your general area of research. Such individuals are often the best at finding flaws and shortcomings that don't pop out for you and others close to the work.

With a final version in hand, you can submit the paper, which today means uploading it to a journal's website. In the rest of this appendix, I answer questions novice writers often ask about submitting manuscripts for publication and about peer review.

> *I've got months of effort invested in my dissertation. Can I submit it for publication after I've reformatted it for a journal?*

No! Dissertations and manuscripts submitted for publication serve different purposes.[1] A dissertation is designed to convince a few people that you have the scientific qualifications to merit a PhD. An article submitted for publication is intended to announce a new scientific result to many scientists, potentially numbering in the thousands. Due to these differing aims, a dissertation is typically much longer (often including a particularly long chapter titled "Review of the Literature") and may include weaker experiments (i.e., experiments that didn't work out as planned and are best thought of as preliminary research that sets the stage for the "main event").

You absolutely need to revise a dissertation—often extensively—before submitting it to a journal. For starters, you need a much shorter Introduction: You don't need to dazzle the reader with your mastery of the literature (only your committee cares about that). Instead, just provide the essential arguments that establish the rationale for your work (see Lesson 5). And report only the main experiment(s), not the preliminary studies that helped you devise the best way to research your topic.

---

[1] These comments apply to a traditional dissertation (or thesis) that includes several chapters devoted to, for example, an Introduction, a Review of the Literature, and descriptions of multiple experiments. Some departments allow students to submit a series of published articles as a dissertation, and my comments don't apply to that format.

My manuscript is done, and I'm ready to submit. How do I select a journal?

Several factors should influence your choice. First, consider journals where other papers on this topic have been published (many of which you probably cite). Second, look at a journal's editorial staff to see whether any of the editors (or associate editors) is an expert on your topic. If you submit to this journal, feel free to request that editor. However, sometimes this strategy can backfire because an editor disqualifies himself or herself due to a conflict of interest (e.g., if your work is either very critical of or highly supportive of the editor's work).

Third, find the journal's impact factor, which is one measure of a journal's influence on the field.[2] Try to decide whether your findings are exceptional and might merit publication in a top-tier journal (one with a high impact factor). Of course, young scientists often have trouble evaluating the impact of their results; this comes with experience. Until you have that experience, ask colleagues who are established authors to help you judge whether your findings seem to belong in a top-tier or midlevel journal. And there's nothing wrong with publishing an occasional paper in a journal with a relatively low impact factor. But if you publish there often and don't publish papers in better journals, you may gain a reputation of doing lots of work that isn't very good.

Journal websites often allow authors to suggest preferred reviewers. Is it really okay to list people here?

Yes, definitely. Authors often are familiar with experts in their area of research and editors appreciate the suggestions. Of course, editors do not always use the suggested reviewers, because the individuals have reviewed for the journal recently or their previous reviews have not been particularly helpful.

When you list suggested reviewers, be sure you do not include individuals who would have a conflict of interest, such as a mentor or student, a colleague, or a recent collaborator (where *recent* is often defined as within the past 5 years). Anyone who might benefit—even slightly—if your paper were to be published should not be listed. Listing such people often suggests to an editor that you're naïve about peer review (best case) or trying to subvert the process (worst case) by stacking the deck in your favor.

---

[2]An impact factor represents a ratio of the number of times articles in a journal are cited by other papers divided by the number of articles published in the journal. Journals with a large impact factor (e.g., 4 or greater in most areas of psychological science) publish a large number of influential papers (as indicated by the fact that they are cited often). In contrast, journals with a small impact factor (e.g., ~1) publish many papers that aren't influential.

Journals typically allow you to list "nonpreferred reviewers," and you should feel free to list a few individuals who you fear might provide biased views of your work. But don't list more than two or three such people because then it may seem as if you're trying to skew the reviewer pool in your favor. Of course, occasionally there's an entire school of thought that opposes the views you present. In that case, it's better to describe the situation in a cover letter instead of listing legions of nonpreferred reviewers.

The editor invited me to submit a revised manuscript, but I don't understand all of the editor's requests for the revision. (Or I disagree with some of them.) Should I contact the editor?

Absolutely. When editors invite a revision, they suggest changes they hope will address the reviewers' concerns and produce a publishable manuscript. If you don't understand those suggestions (or are concerned they won't work), feel free to e-mail the editor. (Do this within 7 to 10 days of receiving the decision e-mail so that the editor doesn't need to reconstruct the thinking behind those suggestions.) Most editors would much prefer answering questions instead of receiving a revision that isn't what they had in mind. That said, don't expect editors to lead you through every step of a revision. Editors are not supposed to act as coauthors (or ghostwriters), and many are adamant about not appearing to vet a revised manuscript before it's submitted.

Why are manuscripts rejected?

Possible reasons include the following. (1) The work has methodological shortcomings and consequently doesn't shed light on the issues it was designed to address. (2) The results are too weak for them to lead to strong conclusions, typically because too many expected outcomes are not significant statistically. (3) The work isn't sufficiently innovative or novel. Editors want to publish discoveries that advance science, not minor variations on prior findings.

I think the reviews are wrong and that my paper should not have been rejected. Should I appeal the decision?

Maybe. An appeal is reasonable if two conditions are met. First, the reviewer's comment needs to be wrong, not just say something with which you disagree. Examples of mistakes in a review are citing the literature incorrectly (e.g., claiming a previously published article showed X when it actually showed Y) or suggesting different kinds of analyses that really aren't appropriate. Second, read the editor's decision e-mail carefully and confirm that the flawed comments contributed to the editor's decision. In other words, a reviewer may be mistaken, but if that mistake didn't contribute to the editor's decision, there's no reason to appeal.

If you decide to appeal, always wait at least 48 hours so that the anger or annoyance associated with the decision can dissipate. But editors will be grateful if you appeal within a week so their thinking about the manuscript will be fresh in mind and they won't have to reconstruct everything.

If my manuscript is rejected, should I submit it to another journal?

Maybe. Start by rereading the reviews. If they point to fundamental flaws in the rationale, methods, or results, there's not much point in sending the manuscript elsewhere. Reviewers at another journal are likely to identify the same flaws, and you'll have wasted everyone's time (yours, the reviewers', and the editor's). However, if the manuscript was rejected because the work didn't break sufficient new ground or the findings didn't provide ironclad evidence for your hypotheses, then consider sending the manuscript to another journal, perhaps one that's not as selective. If it's rejected by a second and third journal, you should accept the fact that this manuscript isn't worthy of publication. Use the reviewers' comments to improve your work and submit a manuscript that tells a more compelling story.

Glossary

Antimetabole—a figure of speech in which emphasis is created by repeating words within a clause but in the reverse order.

These findings indicate that when people love to cheat, they may cheat on those they love.

Dependent clause—a group of words that includes a subject and a verb but that cannot stand alone as a complete sentence; also known as a subordinate clause.

Although these results contradict previous findings in the literature, our view is that the contradiction is more apparent than real.

Hedge—a word (typically an adverb, adjective, or verb) used to convey caution.

This evidence *seems* to lead to the conclusion that . . .

Hyperbole—a figure of speech in which an exaggerated statement is used for emphasis; not recommended for scientific writing because readers may interpret the statement literally.

The literature on face perception is filled with billions of studies.

Independent clause—a group of words that includes a subject and a verb and that can stand alone as a complete sentence; also known as a main clause.

Although these results contradict previous findings in the literature, *our view is that the contradiction is more apparent than real*.

Intensifier—a word (typically an adverb, adjective, or verb) used to convey emphasis.

This evidence *clearly* leads to the conclusion that . . .

Metaphor—a figure of speech in which two dissimilar things are compared implicitly.

For individuals who are depressed, occasional happy experiences *drown in a sea of negative affect*.

Nominalization—a noun derived from a verb or adjective.

significance (from the adjective *significant*), *personification* (from the verb *personify*)

Noun phrase—a group of words including a noun or pronoun that work together as a noun (e.g., as the subject or object of a sentence).

exogenous spatial attention (*exogenous* and *spatial* are adjectives, *attention* is a noun)

Passive voice—a grammatical construction in which the subject of the sentence is a noun that would be the object in a sentence written in active voice.

Longitudinal studies have been conducted by scientists to determine whether . . . (The noun phrase *longitudinal studies* is the object of the verb *have been conducted*)

Prepositional phrase—a group of words that begins with a preposition and usually ends with a noun or pronoun.

Training ended *after the first errorless trial*.

Relative pronoun—a pronoun used to introduce a dependent clause; *that, which, who, whom,* and *whose* are common examples.

This finding was unexpected and suggests *that* previous findings may be spurious.

Simile—a figure of speech in which two dissimilar things are compared explicitly, using *like* or *as*.

On tapping tasks, young children's pace is variable, *like a broken metronome*.

Topic sentence—a sentence that is usually the first sentence in a paragraph and introduces the idea of the paragraph by including a topic and a controlling idea about that topic.

Individuals with low self-control are more likely to make sacrifices for their spouses and partners. (topic = Individuals with low self-control; controlling idea = they are more likely to make sacrifices for their spouses and partners)

Understatement—a figure of speech in which a description is deliberately less strong than the facts or conditions warrant; not recommended for scientific writing because readers may interpret the statement literally.

People recalled pictures somewhat more accurately than words (when in fact they recalled 90% of pictures but only 10% of words)

Verb phrase—a group of words including a main verb and one or more helping verbs.

Many scientists have reported findings . . . (*reported* is the main verb, *have* is the helping verb)

References

Kendall, P. C., Silk, J. S., & Chu, B. C. (2000). Introducing your research report: Writing the introduction. In R. J. Sternberg (Ed.), *Guide to publishing in psychology journals* (pp. 41–57). Cambridge, England: Cambridge University Press.

Plotnik, A. (2007). *Spunk and bite: A writer's guide to bold, contemporary style.* New York: Random House Reference.

Williams, J. M. (2000). *Style: Ten lessons in clarity and grace* (6th ed.). New York: Longman.

Index

Made in the USA
Columbia, SC
27 August 2023

22176818R00085